InnoMaginate!

Turn Yesterday's Products into Tomorrow's Revenue

Traci Robinson-Williams

Claroti, Inc.

Disclaimer

While every effort has been made to ensure the accuracy and usefulness of this material, this book is for informational purposes only and does not constitute legal, tax, accounting, or other professional advice. The author and publisher make no representations or warranties as to the completeness or suitability of the content and shall not be liable for any loss or damages arising from its use. Readers should consult qualified professionals before acting on any ideas in this book. No part of this book may be reproduced or transmitted in any form without prior written permission, except as permitted by law.

For bulk orders and speaking inquiries, contact traci@claroti.com.

tracirobinsonwilliams.com

www.claroti.com

11710 Plaza America Drive, Suite 2000 #4

Reston, VA 20190

Printed in the United States of America

First digital edition 2025. First print edition 2026.

Contents

Dedication

This book is dedicated to my beloved husband
and unwavering cheerleader, Mark,
to all my children,
and to my little sparks of joy
(Logan, Eden, Taylor, Princeton, Micah & Jeremiah).
May your imaginations always carry you beyond
what others say it is possible to achieve.

And in memory of my mother
who believed in me,
to Danielle P. who helped me
InnoMaginate the first time
and to dream of doing it forever,
and to Cassi L. who never got the chance
to write her own book.

"Oh the places you'll go!
There is fun to be done!
There are points to be scored.
There are games to be won.
And the magical things
you can do with that ball
will make you the winning-est
winner of all."

—— Dr. Seuss
Oh, The Places You'll Go!

INTRODUCTION

Welcome to ***InnoMaginate!***

First, thank you for picking up this book, for choosing to lead differently, and for being open to reimagining what growth and innovation can look like in times of uncertainty and constraint.

You're not just here to read. You're here because you know something has to change...and fast! You feel it in your gut and you see it everywhere around you. The market is shifting, the old playbooks aren't working, and waiting for clarity isn't a strategy. It's a risk.

That's why I wrote this book.

In today's environment of policy-driven volatility, inflationary pressure, geopolitical instability, and cautious customer sentiment, innovation can't be optional. It has to be practical. Profitable. Now.

A Note for CMOs and Growth Leaders

If you're a Marketing or Growth leader who's tired of being brought in at the end of the organizational conveyor belt to "make it pretty," this book is for you.

If you're done waiting for your organization to give you a seat at the table—and you are ready to take one—this book is for you.

And if you are an executive that recognizes you need to look at your existing business with fresh eyes, possibly with the intent to increase valuation for a future exit, this book is for you.

InnoMagination™ was built for leaders just like you.

Leaders who don't just want to shape strategy, but who are ready to drive it and lead change.

Marketing is no longer a function. It's a FORCE.

You sit at the intersection of customer insight, brand storytelling, revenue strategy, and cross-functional alignment. You already hold the keys to growth and innovation—you just need the framework to unlock it.

This book gives you that framework. So you can stop reacting and start leading. Not as the team that launches campaigns—but as the team that launches real revenue growth.

What Is *InnoMagination™*?

InnoMagination **is a strategic framework that empowers leaders to drive revenue growth and impact by reimagining the value of existing products, services, and capabilities.**

Built specifically for CMOs and senior Marketing and Growth executives, it offers a clear, five-phase process to identify untapped opportunities, align cross-functional teams, and develop market-ready business cases that influence direction—not just execution. ***InnoMagination*** operates in the middle ground between short-term operational strategy and longer-term innovation strategy.

This is not a support tool. It's a leadership mindshift.

InnoMagination gives Marketing and Growth leaders the process to shape strategy, steer innovation, modernize the Marketing function, and spark momentum across the business—with the insight, influence, and clarity your role demands.

If you're ready to stop waiting for a seat at the table, ***InnoMagination*** gives you the framework to claim it—and the credibility to lead from it.

Why Me? Why This?

I'm a strategist, builder, pattern spotter, and former Marketing leader who's spent over 25 years navigating the trenches of technology, consulting, and communications inside Fortune 50 giants, SaaS startups, and niche players alike.

And here's what I've learned:

The most powerful innovations don't require a blank check.

They require a bold imagination, strategic pattern recognition, and courageous collaboration.

So I built the ***InnoMagination*** framework to teach visionary Marketing and Growth leaders like you how to reignite stalled revenue and activate innovation from within, without waiting for "new."

No massive R&D budgets. No big gambles. And no disrupting your core.

Just fast, low CapEx, de-risked growth, sparked by the assets, capabilities, and teams you already have.

Where It All Began: From Frustration to $1B Growth

I didn't set out to build a framework. I set out to solve a problem that many Marketing and Growth leaders know all too well.

I was tired of being handed a finished product and told to "make it pretty."

Tired of being brought in at the end of the process—after the vision had already been defined, the product built, the budget spent—and then expected to apply polish, positioning, and spin.

Certainly not because I didn't have more to give. But because no one had invited me to give it.

And I know now, I wasn't alone. Maybe you've felt that way, too.

Then came the call...an offer to lead Marketing for the government division of Verizon Wireless. On paper, it looked like a step back from the work I had been doing. But a single conversation reframed everything.

"You're not selling phones," my soon-to-be boss told me. "You're selling tomorrow's capabilities. You'd be helping enable the people who make the world safer and stronger."

It suddenly clicked. Here was an audience that needed very real solutions for very critical problems. And that clarity and mission sparked a question that changed everything.

"What if...
Marketing could LEAD—and not just promote—
strategic innovation?"

So I chose then to stop waiting for the assignment. I assumed the role no one had formally handed me.

And what followed became one of the most defining stories of my career.

A repositioned, reimagined market offer.

A $5M Marketing budget.

Resulting in a $1B revenue engine and a 20,000% ROI.

And an entire industry forced to follow our lead.

That was the moment I realized this wasn't a one-time success. It was a repeatable pattern.

That pattern became a process.

That process became the ***InnoMagination*** framework.

InnoMagination™ **: The Intersection of Marketing, Management Consulting, and Innovation**

InnoMagination isn't just another innovation framework. It's the strategic intersection and synthesis of three powerful business disciplines: Marketing, Management Consulting, and Innovation.

From Marketing, ***InnoMagination*** borrows deep customer understanding, strategic positioning, and compelling storytelling, transforming insight into influence and clarity into revenue.

From Management Consulting, it leverages structured analysis, refined frameworks, strategic decision-making processes, and executive-level business case rigor, ensuring clear insight, credibility, and measurable results.

From Innovation, it takes creativity, bold thinking, rapid experimentation, and agile adaptation, accelerating results in the middle ground of the innovation timeline (6-24 months) while intentionally reducing risk.

If you've worked extensively in any one of these disciplines, you'll encounter fresh tools, perspectives, and best practices from the others in the pages ahead. No matter your background, InnoMagination will expand your toolkit, sharpen your strategic thinking, and unleash new opportunities you might never have imagined.

When Marketing discipline meets Management Consulting rigor and Innovation creativity, extraordinary results follow—rapidly, repeatedly, and profitably.

That intersection is exactly where ***InnoMagination*** lives.

What This Book Offers You

In the following pages, I am going to show you WHY you need InnoMagination, the paradigm shift that demonstrates HOW Marketing and Growth can lead, and HOW you can step up and take charge.

This book is both an invitation and a challenge:

To **SEE** overlooked possibilities in your business.

To **SPARK** ideas that align with market shifts.

To **DO** the work that turns constrained resources into catalytic growth

InnoMagination is built for this moment in the market.

For the leader under pressure to grow without overspending.

For teams stretched thin but still hungry to make an impact.

For organizations that can't afford to bet on untested, ungrounded moonshots.

This is innovation with both feet on the ground.

You'll walk away with a practical, proven methodology that helps you uncover what's hiding in plain sight...and turn it into profitable new value before your competitors even see it coming.

How to Use the Reflection Prompts

This isn't a book you just read. It's a book you experience, that you work through with your teams.

These prompts aren't here for decoration...they're transformation tools.

They're designed to spark insight, deepen dialogue, and push you (and your teams) past surface-level thinking.

Here's how to make them effective:

1. Read straight through the whole book first. Let the ideas marinate. Don't stop to dissect—just absorb. Your brain needs the full picture before you start pulling it apart.

2. Then go back, prompt by prompt. This is where the real work begins. Alone first, then with your team. These aren't passive questions. They're built to challenge assumptions and surface what's really driving your decisions.

3. Journal. Discuss. Rumble. These prompts are mirrors and launchpads. Use them to SEE what's true, SPARK what's possible, and DO what matters most.

4. Revisit regularly. Once isn't enough. Growth is a loop, not a line. Your answers will evolve—and that's exactly the point.

So don't rush. Don't gloss over things. Don't skip the deep thinking about how InnoMagination can work for you.

Use the Reflection Prompts to spark the conversations you've been avoiding...and the ones that will change everything.

One Final Ask Before We Begin

I wrote this book for people like you, leaders who refuse to settle for the status quo. So again...please don't read this passively. Engage with these ideas. Share them. Test them. Make them your own.

And know this: ***InnoMagination*** isn't about more ideas, more people, or more budget.

It's all about better execution.

The future belongs to those who can move fast, with focus.

Let's go find the treasure that's just inches beneath your feet. You are so close!

Let's ***InnoMaginate!***

Best,
Traci

ONE

THE INNOVATION WAKE-UP CALL FOR MARKETING AND GROWTH LEADERS

"The riskiest thing we can do is just maintain the status quo."

— Bob Iger

Chapter Objectives:
Redefine innovation for Marketing and Growth leaders. Expose forces sabotaging revenue growth in mature enterprises. Introduce ***InnoMagination™*** *as a repeatable process to reimagine assets, activate value, and lead strategic innovation.*

Innovation shouldn't feel like catching smoke with your bare hands. But for many Marketing and Growth leaders in established enterprises, that's exactly what it feels like—elusive, overcomplicated, and just out of reach.

If you've felt this way, you're not alone. And you're not wrong.

You've been handed legacy systems, conflicting expectations, outdated assumptions, and a culture that quietly (or in some cases, stridently) resists change. And then you're told to "drive revenue growth."

This chapter is your permission slip to walk the halls and challenge it all.

What's keeping you from leading innovation isn't a lack of creativity, insight, or drive. It's the baggage your organization—and frankly, the entire business world—has been carrying around about what innovation really is.

Redefining Innovation

Before we go any further, let's make sure we are on the same page.

Let's properly define innovation: *The process of introducing new or improved ideas, products, services, or ways of working that create value for customers, the business, or both.*

Nowhere in that definition does it say innovation has to be expensive, technical, disruptive, or owned by a separate team. It doesn't require a lab coat, a billion-dollar budget, or a three-year roadmap.

It requires **creating value.** THAT'S IT.

And as a Marketing or Growth leader, you're positioned better than **anyone** to activate innovation. In fact, you are UNIQUELY positioned in the organization for this. You have the deep product knowledge (probably better than anyone other than Product or Engineering), you are singularly attuned to the market insights, and YOU run the engine that can bring this all to life.

What are you waiting for?? Honestly, if your organization doesn't have a chief strategy officer, just give yourself the *de facto* role until somebody tells you to stop!

That is, unless you WANT to continue to wait for permission to lead, to wait for the handouts, to wait for an invitation to be the driver of transformation (ha!) that you know is necessary for your organization's survival. In most cases, that invitation isn't coming.

So take it.

You have the power to choose. To imagine a role that is bigger, more strategic, more IMPACTFUL than you have right now.

Go reinvent yourself as a key innovator!

This book will show you what you need to do.

The Myths That Keep You Stuck

Despite what you've been told, innovation doesn't have to be:

- **Expensive:** Some of the most effective innovations come from rethinking what already exists. Small, strategic shifts in customer experience, messaging, packaging, business model, or delivery can transform an existing product or service into a renewed source of value.

- **Tech-driven**: Technology is a tool, not the definition of innovation. True innovation is about solving real problems in better ways. Technology is only the enabler.

- **Big & Transformational**: Small, focused moves can drive massive returns. As Peter Sims[1] puts it in *"Little Bets"*, small, iterative changes can unlock disproportionate impact with minimal risk. (Tip: Lessons learned from the DevOps and Agile development worlds—Start small. Ideate. Experiment. Learn fast. Iterate. Scale wisely.)

- **Someone else's job:** Innovation doesn't live in a lab. It lives and breathes in insight, proximity to the customer, and the courage to act. When everyone sees innovation as part of their role and responsibility, it becomes part of the culture.

- **Resource-laden:** You don't need more people. You need more focus, a process, and clarity from the research, insights, and direction you gain. As Scott Anthony, Professor at Tuck School of Business, advises, innovation doesn't require a team of creatives. It simply needs a framework that allows anyone to contribute meaningfully.[2]

And here's the big one:

- **Risky**: The real risk is doing nothing while your competitors evolve. Risk comes from ignoring reality, not from innovating with intention. You can mitigate risk by starting with what already works, testing refinements, and iterating based on evidence you collect along the way.

Don't let outdated myths keep you from seeing what's right in front of you.

Like a tiny hinge on a large door, in innovation, it's often the smallest reimagining—of a product, a message, a model, or a market—that opens the door to the biggest opportunities.

The Pressure Cooker CMOs Are Living In

Let's not sugarcoat it. If you're leading Marketing, especially an organization in the late-growth, maturity, or renewal phases of the business lifecycle, you're operating in a storm of:

- Geopolitical instability
- Economic uncertainty [3, 4]
- Talent shortages [3]
- Technology disruption [5]
- Commoditization [5]
- Sustainability demands
- Complexity at scale

You're expected to deliver growth, protect the brand, lead digital transformation, and make the quarter—all while navigating headwinds that your predecessors never had to face.

And yet, innovation is now table stakes. It's no longer optional.

It's your survival strategy!

What Happens If You Wait?

You might be tempted to finish this book and wait.

Wait for more budget. Wait for a clearer market. Wait for someone to greenlight something "big enough to matter."

Unfortunately, there's a dangerous and painful reality. **The cost of "wait and see" is no longer neutral. Doing nothing can cost you more than you imagine.**

You lose time.
You lose out on potential revenue.
You lose market relevance.
You lose the path to internal wins your team is desperate for.

InnoMagination™ exists because waiting for the "perfect moment" is what got many companies into trouble in the first place.

Please, I beseech you—don't wait. Start where you are. Start with what you already have.

The Hidden Threats Inside Your Organization
The real blockers to innovation aren't "out there." They're baked into the culture, systems, and expectations of your business.

Time Poverty
Day-to-day operations are consuming leadership bandwidth. C-suite leaders are stuck in the now, with little space to think about what's next.

The tyranny of quarterly reporting creates a hamster wheel of short-term focus, leaving little room for strategic foresight or innovation investment.

Fear of Failure & Risk Paralysis
In many later stage organizations, the culture doesn't just discourage risk—it actively punishes it.

It's not that people don't want to innovate. It's that the systems they operate in make failure professionally expensive. Compensation is tied to performance metrics that reward predictability. Promotions go to those who play it safe. And public missteps—no matter how well-intentioned —can follow a leader for years.

The result? Even smart, exceptionally capable leaders make a quiet, rational calculation: The risk isn't worth the reward.

Why stick your neck out when the potential upside is vague, but the downside is career-limiting?

This creates a culture of learned paralysis, where the unspoken rule becomes, 'Don't be the one who fails. Don't be the one who tries.'

Consequently, no one dares to lead.

Innovation inherently involves risk (then again, so does NOT doing anything, but more on that later...). In many organizations, the fear of getting it wrong outweighs the desire to try.

Executives worry about cannibalizing revenue. Teams fear reputational damage. Everyone is waiting for someone else to take the first swing.

This creates a culture of hesitation. And hesitation kills innovation.

You need to de-risk the work culturally, not just financially.

Celebrate smart risks. Reward strategic failure. Make learning part of the scorecard, not just winning.

Spanx® founder Sara Blakely tells of how her father asked her each evening over dinner, *"How did you fail today?"* The expectation was that, if you aren't failing, you aren't trying. And my own father used to say, *"If you don't swing the bat, you can never hit the ball."*

Give your people the safety net to attempt new things without fear.

The Pressure to Invent Instead of Reimagine

Too many leaders are chasing the next big thing while overlooking the untapped potential of what's already in front of them.

Think like Adobe®. When faced with the technology trend of cloud adoption, the company foresaw the opportunity to increase revenue stability and predictability while combating software piracy, increasing customer engagement and retention, and accelerating a faster path to regular innovation releases. It didn't build new software; it reimagined how customers accessed it by shifting to a subscription model.

The company went from $4.4 billion in annual revenue in 2012 to $12.87 billion in 2020, nearly tripling its revenue in eight years. [6]

Your organization is full of assets, products, and processes that could be revitalized with a fresh lens. But if your team is only rewarded for "new," they'll miss the value in "next."

Internal Innovation Gridlock

Your innovation process shouldn't feel like a legal review.

Unfortunately, in many organizations, even small ideas are forced through a maze of approvals, competing priorities, and bureaucratic inertia.

The result? Delays. Frustration. Missed windows.

Innovation doesn’t die because it isn't good. It dies because it gets trapped and can’t break out.

Simplify the structure. Shorten the cycle. Allow experiments. Empower the teams.

The *Legacy Lock Contradiction*

Efficiency is the enemy of agility.

Ponder that for a minute. It sounds like a paradox, but it really is true.

The very systems that made your business scalable—hierarchies, standardization, optimization—are now the ones slowing innovation to a crawl.

This is the Legacy Lock Contradiction:
“Your company is perfectly optimized for what was, not for what’s next.”

At some point in your company’s journey, predictability, repeatability, and risk management became the primary levers for growth. And for good reason—those systems helped you scale. But over time, they calcify. What once made you strong becomes what makes you slow.

Here’s how it shows up:
Approval chains get longer.
Budget gates get tighter.
Decision rights become murky.
Innovation teams are treated as outsiders instead of integrators.

And suddenly, everyone's "supporting innovation," but no one is actually doing it.

The result? You're preserving the past at the cost of the future. You've built a machine that's excellent at protecting what you already know how to deliver—but terrible at exploring what you could create next.

But there is good news. **You don't have to blow up the machine.**

You need a second motion; a parallel rhythm inside the business that's designed for speed, experimentation, and evolution.

A motion that:
Moves faster than the annual planning cycle.
Tests early instead of launching late.
Builds belief across teams through small wins, not massive initiatives.
Protects space for bold thinking without disrupting core business operations.

Think of it as creating an "innovation lane" that runs alongside the core business, not in opposition to it. ***InnoMagination*** gives you the process to do exactly that.

(Tip: The future won't wait for your processes and systems to catch up.)

Hidden Asset Blindness
You're sitting on diamonds and you don't even know it.
Silos, org charts, and outdated roles keep teams blind to the proprietary technologies, customer insights, internal capabilities, and data that could power your next big move.

Your job as a leader? Break down the walls. Create visibility. Encourage cross-functional collaboration that surfaces what's been hiding in plain sight.

Innovation often lives between the boxes on your org chart. Don't be afraid to let the silos bleed together. Let the people and the ideas mix freely.

Market Misalignment

Even great ideas can fail if they don't meet a real need.

Too many teams build in isolation, driven by what's possible, not what's valuable. If your innovation isn't grounded in evolving customer behavior and market opportunity, it's a mirage.

Get closer to the customer.

Validate early. Iterate fast. Stay aligned with what the market is actually asking for.

The Speed-to-Market Conundrum

Being first isn't everything...but being late is a massive liability.

Traditional innovation cycles are too slow for modern markets. By the time your great idea clears approvals, someone else already owns the space.

The answer? First-scaler advantage.

Use your existing infrastructure to move faster than the startups, effectively commercializing, operationalizing, and achieving widespread adoption at scale. Streamline decision-making. Build for speed. Launch in beta if you must, but for goodness sake, just launch already!

In the words of Winston Churchill, *"Perfection is the enemy of progress."*

Rigid Resource Allocation

Budgeting models built for predictability are poorly suited for innovation.

If your innovation team is begging for scraps while the core business gets everything it needs, don't be surprised when no new value makes it to market.

Set aside flexible funds for innovation throughout the organization, a small "Tinker Fund" of sorts. Create lightweight governance. Make room for discovery, not just delivery.

Cultural Inertia

This one's invisible...and oh-so-dangerous.

When teams have been conditioned to prioritize consistency over creativity, innovation feels unsafe. When collaboration is rare and risk is punished, innovation becomes someone else's job.

The old maxim is true. Culture is not what you ***say*** it is. It's what you ***reward***.

If you want innovation to thrive, create a culture where curiosity is internal currency. Where collaboration is the default. Where the *status quo* is challenged, not worshipped.

Why Marketing Is Positioned to Lead (But Often Doesn't)

You're on the front lines of insight. You hear the customer first. You see shifts in behavior before the rest of the org catches up.

And yet, Marketing is too often brought in at the end of the corporate assembly line to "make it pretty" instead of helping to define strategic direction at the beginning of the process. That has ALWAYS pissed me off! What a waste of the immense talent and potential overflowing in the Marketing function!

That's not just a missed opportunity. It's a strategic tragedy.

Marketing, when empowered with the right process, can lead innovation—not just wrap it up in a pretty bow.

You already have the pieces. Now you just need (to give yourself) permission and a process to do this.

The Middle Ground:
Innovation's Most Overlooked Opportunity

Most organizations obsess over two timelines: Now and Next-Next.

They focus on short-term wins—this quarter's revenue, this year's campaign metrics. Or they chase long-term big bets...AI labs, the "Future of" everything, etc.

But there's a critical, often ignored space in between: **The Middle Ground.** The 6–24 month window where ***InnoMagination*** lives.

It's not urgent enough to dominate the next board meeting. It's not sexy enough to land in the long-term innovation portfolio. But it's where revenue growth is hiding—right now.

And it's where Marketing and Growth leaders have the clearest paths to lead.

This is the space where you get to:

- **Reposition** existing offerings for new segments or use cases
- **Repackage** capabilities through new models or bundles or configurations
- **Refresh** messaging, look, feel, UX, or features to capture emerging demand
- **Rethink** your footprint, expand into adjacent markets without starting from scratch, or re-evaluate processes
- **Reimagine** overlooked assets into revenue-generating platforms

- **Realign** tactical execution with organizational strategy

The Middle Ground is where reimagination meets reality. It's where you can make bold moves—without needing massive budgets, new infrastructure, or five-year bets.

It's also where you can build credibility, influence strategy, and deliver measurable ROI while other teams are still mapping out their long-term innovation timelines.

If you've ever felt stuck between the urgent and the unattainable, this is your call to take the reins.

The Middle Ground isn't a gap. It's a growth lane. And it's wide open.

Introducing *InnoMagination™*

InnoMagination is a strategic framework built for Marketing and Growth leaders in later-stage organizations who are ready to stop reacting and start steering.

It gives you a clear, five-phase process to:

- **SEE** hidden opportunities in your existing portfolio
- **SPARK** alignment across cross-functional teams
- **DO** the work that drives growth without waiting for permission

This isn't theory. It's a system proven in Fortune 50 environments, designed to help you shift mindset, build momentum, and deliver measurable results—starting with what you already have.

Your Role Has Changed. Your Frameworks Should, Too

You're expected to:

- Translate customer insight into revenue
- Align teams around a shared vision
- Defend the brand while accelerating growth
- Be bold, fast, and accountable
- And somehow—make it all look effortless

The old playbooks just won't get you there anymore.

But you're not stuck. You're ready.

Final Thought: Innovation Isn't Optional. It's Your Advantage.

You don't need more time. You don't need more people. You need a smarter way to lead innovation inside the business you already have.

InnoMagination gives you that path.

So if you're tired of being brought in at the end...If you're done waiting for permission to lead...If you know there's more potential inside your team, your brand, your business...

Then this isn't just a book. It's your moment.

See. Spark. Do. Let's ***InnoMaginate™*** what's next.

Reflection Prompts for Leaders

Use these prompts to turn insights into action:

- How have these beliefs shaped our approach to innovation, even unintentionally?
- Are we reinforcing a culture of risk aversion that limits innovation?
- Where are we rewarding behaviors that kill innovation?
- What's one internal assumption about innovation we need to challenge today?
- What's one structural or cultural shift we can make in the next 30 days to unlock momentum?

Two

The Evolving Strategy Imperative for CMOs

"It is not necessary to change. Survival is not mandatory."

— W. Edwards Deming

Chapter Objective: *Define the evolving mandate of CMO roles—shifting from functional leadership to enterprise growth ownership—and outline the strategic capabilities required to lead with impact in a high-pressure, data-driven landscape.*

The role of the CMO is being rewritten in real time.

Today's CMOs are no longer evaluated solely on creative vision, brand leadership, or market insight. They're now expected to drive strategic growth, generate revenue, and guide the business through turbulence, with both eyes on the customer and both feet planted firmly in the numbers.

This is no longer simply about owning your function. This is where the 'ART of Marketing' meets the 'SCIENCE of Marketing' in real-time.

The new mandate requires owning the ***outcomes***...and everyone is accountable.

The Shift: From Function to Growth Leadership

Once seen as the 'defender of the brand' or 'driver of demand', the CMO is now expected to be an 'enterprise growth leader', a visible, accountable driver of revenue strategy across the business. The role of the CMO isn't just evolving, it's expanding at an incredible rate. Deloitte identifies four core mandates shaping the future of marketing leadership: *Growth Driver, Innovation Catalyst, Brand Storyteller, and Capability Builder.*[8]

Your C-suite peers are ready for this evolution—expecting it actually. But only 26% of CMOs feel confident in their ability to impact all four areas.[8] That gap? It's not just worries about skillset. Rather, it's related to mindset, momentum, and stepping into a new kind of leadership.

CMOs are facing pressure to break out of their traditional silos and step into a role that unifies strategy, operational aspects, customer experience, and innovation.

This is what the modern market demands:

- Cross-functional fluency
- Strategic agility
- Revenue accountability
- Clear impact

None of this is optional. It's the new baseline for expectation...and performance.

Short-Term Pressure, Long-Term Responsibility

A recent survey shows that "nearly 75% of surveyed CMOs cited short-term company commercial growth as their most pressing priority for the next 12-18 months, *above longer-term goals*".[9] That's not a failure of leadership, it's a reflection of the environment.

Budgets are tightening, expectations are rising, and timelines are shrinking.

All of this creates a terrific tension and challenge. You know you can't build sustainable growth on short-term thinking alone. Somehow, you must master the art of balancing immediate revenue impact with long-term brand and business value.

This is where strategic tension becomes strategic power...if you know how to manage it well.

The New Mandate: Revenue, Not Just Reach

You're now in the hot seat when it comes to revenue generation. Yet, 71% of CMOs say they struggle with insufficient budget to execute even their core digital strategies.[10]

This isn't just frustrating. It's unsustainable.

To survive and thrive, you must:

- Translate marketing strategy into business outcomes
- Build stronger, faster GTM engines
- Prove ROI with data, not just attribution models
- Shift from 'brand steward' to 'business driver'

This is the transformation fueled by **Marketing Powered Innovation**, where Marketing doesn't just promote growth, it creates it. (We'll talk more about this in Chapter 6.)

Data as a Strategic Weapon

You are now expected to go far beyond intuition or past experience. Like it or not, we're in the era of data-backed, insight-fueled, customer-driven decision-making.

That means leading teams that:

- Leverage advanced analytics
- Build and optimize MarTech stacks (and integrate AI as a productivity maximizer)
- Close internal skills gaps
- Personalize customer experiences at scale
- Use data to guide innovation, not just justify it

With AI becoming mainstream, the demand (read "expectation") for intelligent, adaptive marketing strategies is higher than ever. The ability to turn insight into action as part of your routine workflows is what separates static functions from strategic engines.

Digital Transformation as a Leadership Imperative

Seventy-percent of CEOs believe AI will significantly impact how value is created in their organizations soon.[11]

It's essential to recognize that the adoption of AI and other technologies isn't just about new tools. They must be integrated into the way you operate and used to support your strategic direction.

Now, YOU must lead the charge on digital transformation by:

- Orchestrating cross-functional adoption
- Aligning new tech with customer experience strategy
- Ensuring internal capability matches external ambition

It's essential to build innovation into the system and not tack it on as an after-thought.

Collaboration is the New Power Skill

Only 54% of CMOs feel their value is fully understood by decision-makers across the C-suite.[12]

And with the average tenure of a CMO "lower than the most common C-suite roles other than chief operating officer", that could be more than simply a perception problem; it may be a relevance problem.[13]

CEOs are raising the bar for CMOs...and many aren't measuring up. According to Gartner (2025), only 27% of CEOs and CFOs felt their CMO exceeded expectations last year, and just 34% are aligned with CMOs on how Marketing should fuel growth. And that kind of disconnect isn't just a performance issue—it's a strategic business (and career) risk.[14]

Those are pretty frightening statistics for CMOs and Marketing leaders.

To stay in play, it is absolutely essential for you to:

- Collaborate across lines of business
- Align KPIs with organizational goals
- Create shared ownership of growth outcomes
- Build trust through transparency, not turf wars

In a flat, fast-moving market, no one wins alone. And no function can afford to operate in isolation.

The Real Balancing Act

Forty-five percent of CEOs are concerned their business won't be viable in 10 years if current strategies continue.[15]

This creates a real tension: CMOs must drive performance today while building resilience for tomorrow.

That means:

- Investing in the brand while driving demand
- Prioritizing experiments while protecting cash
- Scaling what works without sacrificing what matters

This dual lens of performance AND resilience is what makes modern Marketing leadership so valuable and so complex.

The New CMO Playbook

The message is crystal clear. You're not just leading a department...you're ***architecting growth***.

In this emerging world, titles are less important than outcomes. Growth can't be in a silo.

What matters is your ability to:

- ***See*** the market and the opportunity clearly
- ***Spark*** change cross-functionally by aligning the organization courageously
- ***Do*** the work that drives value—and do it fast

The most successful Marketing leaders will be those who *embrace the evolution*, not as a burden, but as a breakthrough.

The future of your organization isn't waiting for the market to calm down.

It's waiting for you to lead differently.

Reflection Prompts for Leaders

Use these prompts to turn insight into action:

- Am I operating as a functional expert or as a strategic growth leader?
- Where am I still prioritizing tactics over impact?
- How well am I collaborating across the C-suite to drive unified outcomes?
- How can I balance today's performance with tomorrow's innovation without losing either?
- What's one shift I can make this quarter to align my team more closely with organizational strategy?

THREE

REALIZING INNOVATION ISN'T (ALWAYS) ABOUT A NEW TOY

"Uncommon thinkers reuse what common thinkers refuse."

—J.R.D. Tata

Chapter Objective: *Demonstrate how reimagining existing assets—not chasing new tech—can unlock powerful innovation, proving that mindset, alignment, and storytelling often matter more than invention.*

Let me let you in on a little secret.

When I was first recruited to lead government marketing at Verizon Wireless, it didn't feel like a leap forward. I had come from working in cutting-edge technology for high-stakes government clients—and telecom to the government (basically a regulated industry within a regulated industry) felt like a step down. A slower lane. A much less exciting stage.

Honestly, it felt like trading in a Ferrari for a minivan.

But then my soon-to-be boss, who would become a trusted mentor and friend across my career, said something that shifted everything:

> **"You're not selling phones. You're selling tomorrow's capabilities. You'd be helping enable the people who make the world safer and stronger."**

That reframed the opportunity in a single sentence. And in that moment, I saw it:

This wasn't just a job. It was a chance to lead differently. Suddenly, I wasn't just walking into a new position. I was stepping into ***possibility.*** (I find something absolutely MAGICAL in that word!)

What followed wasn't flashy. It was focused.

I did the research and I saw what others hadn't yet seen.

A massive, underserved Public Safety market.

An expiring competitor patent.

A product stack we already had.

A gap no one else had connected.

So I asked the question that would become the spark for everything that came after:

"What if we...?"

I spotted a gap our competitor didn't think we'd fill. And I built a strategy to own it.

I realized we didn't need to create something entirely new. We already had the infrastructure. We had an amazing brand. We had the tech and we had the talent.

So then I moved on it. I built the business case. I sold the vision—upward, sideways, 'slantways', across functions. I brought together Marketing, Product, Legal, Sales, Finance, Government Relations, Public Relations, and other departments and divisions across the company.

And together, we didn't invent something new. We reimagined what already existed.

We launched a national crisis response campaign. We repackaged an offering. We rebuilt the messaging from the ground up. We created a new value story—and then we backed it with relentless execution.

The outcome?

More than $1 billion in revenue over the next ten years.

20,000%+ ROI on an initial $5M Marketing investment.

5,000+ inbound leads representing government and public safety agencies across the nation in year one.

And according to leadership at a competitor company, the entire industry was forced to shift their Go-To-Market strategy because we charted this new course. Years later, a senior executive from one of our biggest competitors told me, "You changed the game. We had to adapt to keep up."

That was the moment I knew.

This wasn't a fluke.

It was a framework. A repeatable, scalable process that could be applied again and again.

And that process became ***InnoMagination™***.

Innovation Isn't a Department. It's a Discipline.

After that, I went on to lead similar Marketing Powered Innovation-type efforts at global tech companies Accenture, GitLab, and other niche firms. Each time, the ingredients were slightly different, but the pattern was the same.

1. SEE the opportunity
2. SPARK the belief
3. DO the work—with what you already have

And every time, the biggest challenge wasn't the market.

It wasn't the competition.

It wasn't the tech.

It was getting people to believe that we already had what we needed to win.

There's Likely an Elephant in Your Budget

Soooo, let's talk about R&D...How much are you investing in it?

And of those investments, how many actually make it to market?

If you're like most mature organizations, the answer is rather uncomfortable.

Millions invested annually, dozens of initiatives launched, a high failure rate, and far too many ideas that quietly die without earning ROI.

Traditional R&D can be expensive, slow, and often disconnected from what the market actually wants right now.

InnoMagination doesn't replace R&D or your Innovation team (it is actually complementary), but it does give you a faster, lower-risk pathway to deliver market value using what you already have.

Think of it as innovation that doesn't need the lab coat.

The Real Work: Shifting Mindsets, Not Just Strategies

This is the part where many Marketing leaders struggle. You're sitting on powerful platforms, brilliant people, and valuable assets. But if your teams can't ***see*** the possibility, they won't move.

That's why ***InnoMagination*** isn't just about systems. It's about storytelling.

You have to paint the picture of ***what could be***.

You have to show people where you're going and ***why*** it matters.

You have to make it ***personal***, so everyone sees their specific role in achieving the win.

I've learned that if you can't inspire people to believe in the potential of what you can accomplish together, they'll default to what's familiar.

That's why I like to bring this quote into the room:

> *"Oh the places you'll go!*
> *There is fun to be done!*
> *There are points to be scored.*
> *There are games to be won.*
> *And the magical things you can do with that ball will make you the winning-est winner of all."* [16]

Yes, it's from Dr. Seuss. And yes, it works—because it reminds people that ***they can win with what they have already been equipped with*** and have fun doing it. AND, that the magic isn't in a shiny new toy. It's in how we use what we already have, together.

Last Thoughts: The Lesson for Leaders

InnoMagination doesn't require a lab or a patent.

It just requires a fresh perspective and a team brave enough to act.

You don't need more tech. You need more alignment. More storytelling. More intention.

You need to show your teams, and yourself, that the future isn't waiting to be invented.

It's waiting to be ***InnoMagined***.

Reflection Prompts for Leaders

Use these prompts to turn insight into action:

- Where in your organization are you underutilizing existing capabilities?
- What segment, customer group, or market opportunity are you overlooking?
- How much of your R&D portfolio from the last three years has failed to launch?
- Are your teams waiting for a "new toy" or being empowered to reimagine what's already in reach?
- What story do you need to tell to spark belief in what's possible?
- Who could benefit from seeing your strategy through the lens of "tomorrow's capabilities"?

FOUR

EUREKA! THE OVERLOOKED DIAMOND MINE IN YOUR PORTFOLIO

"Do not search for success off in the distance, but instead recognize it and grasp it right where you are!"

— Napoleon Hill

Chapter Objective: *Help leaders uncover hidden value within their existing portfolio by shifting focus from chasing what's new to recognizing and reimagining overlooked assets already in their grasp.*

I'm going to be completely transparent about this. I've got a bit of a 'shiny object' problem. You probably do, too. It's natural.

There's always some next big thing. A new trend. A competitor's move. A product that "everyone" says we have to build. It's easy to get swept into the chase, especially when the pressure to innovate and deliver growth is relentless.

But what if the growth you're looking for isn't "out there" at all (wherever 'there' is)?

What if it's been sitting under your feet this whole time?

Let me tell you a story.

The Parable of the Missed Opportunity

Perhaps you've heard of the tale, told hundreds of times by Russell H. Conwell, founder of Temple University, called *"Acres of Diamonds."* Here's the short version:

> *A wealthy farmer hears about the riches of diamond mines and sells his rocky land to go find them. He travels far and wide, searching in vain. Eventually, bankrupt, and heartbroken, he gives up, loses everything, and dies destitute.*
>
> *Meanwhile, the man who bought his farm discovers a large, dirt-encrusted rock in the stream out back, which he eventually learns is an enormous uncut diamond. As it turns out, the land was abundantly rich with diamonds all along, and that farm—the one the original farmer sold—became one of the richest diamond fields ever discovered in that country. The original owner had been sitting on a fortune; he just didn't know how to recognize it.*

The moral of the story? ***We often overlook the value we already own because we're too busy chasing what looks better somewhere else.***

What's in Your Backyard?

Now think about your own portfolio. The products you've already launched. The services you already sell. The customer segments you've already won.

What if you're sitting on untapped value without realizing it?

Untapped potential can take many forms:

- Products with underutilized features
- Customer segments you haven't explored
- Capabilities you haven't marketed or monetized
- Internal data, insights, or IP that haven't been leveraged
- Positioning opportunities you haven't fully owned

In a culture obsessed with "what's next," smart leaders are rediscovering the power of what's ***now***.

CASE STUDY: The 3M® Case of the Sticky Note That Almost Got Stuck

In the late 1960s, a 3M scientist was working on a new kind of adhesive. What he created was...odd. It was low-tack. It didn't bond permanently.

It was, by traditional standards, a failed R&D output.

For years, it sat unused. Unmarketed. Unloved.

Until another employee saw a different use: temporary page markers that wouldn't damage paper.

That "failed" adhesive became one of the most successful office products in history: Post-it® Notes.

The lesson?

It wasn't new R&D that created the breakthrough...

It was seeing differently...*InnoMaginating* what was already there.

InnoMagination **Doesn't Always Mean New**

Let me be abundantly clear. I'm not anti-innovation. I've built my career on innovating and creating new ideas.

The key benefit of ***InnoMagination*** is that it doesn't (usually) require building anything new.

It's about ***seeing*** things differently, unlocking and activating value ***from what already exists***.

> InnoMagination is asking, ***"What are we taking for granted that could become our next growth engine?"***

Sometimes, the biggest breakthroughs come from looking sideways, not forward.

Why We Miss the Diamonds

Typically, there are a few reasons we overlook what's already in front of us.

1. **Familiarity breeds contempt (in a business sense, a better word is probably 'blindness').** When you're close to something, it's easy to stop seeing it clearly...or even at all.

2. **The myth of new = better.** We equate innovation with novelty (and we crave novelty), when the objective is really value.

3. **Lack of internal exploration.** We don't audit or analyze our own portfolio deeply enough.

4. **Under-leveraged collaboration.** Teams don't always talk to each other about what's working, what's not working, and what could be working.

But there's good news, too. Once you know where to look, the opportunities tend to reveal themselves.

We'll spend a lot of time in later chapters on how to dig for diamonds in your own portfolio and start uncovering the value that's already beneath your feet.

Last Thoughts: The Leadership Lesson

So what do we learn from all this?

The original farmer didn't lack ambition. He lacked perspective.

He didn't know how to spot the diamonds in their raw form.

He didn't realize that true wealth often lies in recognizing—*not reinventing*—value.

As a Marketing leader, your job is to help your team SEE what they've stopped seeing.

To SPARK belief in the assets they've grown numb to.

To DO the work that turns overlooked potential into undeniable performance.

You might not need a new product. You might just need a new lens.

Reflection Prompts for Leaders

Use these prompts to turn insight into action:

- What product or service in our portfolio hasn't reached its full potential? Why?
- Are we overlooking growth opportunities because they don't look "new enough"?
- What internal data, insights, or assets are we under-leveraging?
- How often do we audit our portfolio for hidden value?
- What's one "diamond" we can dig up this quarter?

FIVE

WHO STANDS TO GAIN? INNOVATIVE THINKERS VS. THE HISTORICAL FOOTNOTES

"The future of life as we know it is being determined by everything we're doing—and not doing. Now."

— Oprah Winfrey

Chapter Objective: *Contrast companies that embrace innovation with those that resist it, revealing how proactive reinvention versus past success determines who thrives and who fades into irrelevance.*

One of the most dangerous assumptions a company can make is that what made them successful in the past will keep them successful.

It won't.

The companies that become historical footnotes don't fail because they lacked talent, resources, or reputation. They fail because they resisted change, misread the market, or leaned too hard on past glory.

The ability for mature companies to innovate, and renew, isn't just an advantage.

It's a matter of survival.

The Business Maturity Lifecycle

Every business, no matter the industry or size, moves through a predictable lifecycle:

Startup – Establishing presence, validating value →
Growth – Rapid expansion, scaling operations →
Maturity – Plateauing growth, market saturation →
Renewal or Decline – Reinvent (and return to Growth) or fade away

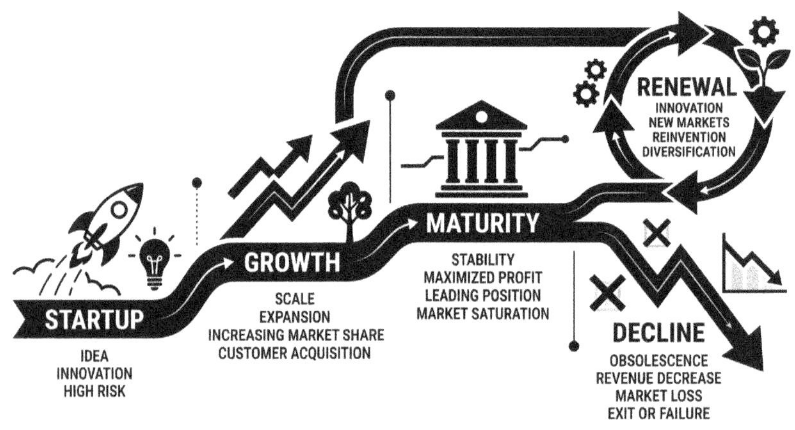

The Business Maturity Lifecycle

The Maturity phase is where many organizations get stuck. At this point, you've stabilized and built brand equity. You're generating predictable revenue. But without continuous innovation, the next phase isn't growth. It's erosion.

This is the turning point. You must pick a path.

It is a choice. You either renew or decline. Doing nothing is a choice.

Decline is characterized by **decreasing market share, declining revenue, declining or negative growth, reduced profitability, and potential**

obsolescence due to emerging technologies and shifting customer preferences.

Do any of these characteristics describe your organization?

To avoid decline, you must invest in new technologies, explore new markets, or reinvent your existing products and services.

What Renewal Looks Like

Let's look at companies that didn't just survive maturity. They reimagined it.

Slack®: From Failed Game to Workplace Essential

Slack wasn't built as a collaboration tool. It was originally an internal communications platform created by a gaming company developing a now-defunct game called Glitch. When the game failed, the team could've folded.

Instead, they recognized the real asset they'd built.

They pivoted. They rebranded. And they launched Slack, reshaping how teams communicate globally.

Slack didn't invent a new idea. It redeployed an overlooked one.[17]

Corning®: From Glassware to Gorilla Glass®

Corning has been around for over 150 years, known originally for its consumer glass and household ceramics. But it didn't cling to its legacy.

Instead, Corning saw the explosion in mobile device usage and recognized a new need—durable, high-quality glass.

Enter Gorilla Glass, which is now used in billions of smartphones.

Corning didn't reinvent its business. It redirected its expertise toward a high-growth market.[18]

IBM®: From Hardware Giant to AI & Cloud Leader

IBM was once synonymous with typewriters and mainframes. But it saw the writing on the wall. Hardware was commoditizing.

Rather than fade, IBM pivoted toward software and services, investing heavily in cloud computing and AI.

Through strategic insight into emerging market trends, IBM was able to adapt its business model effectively and align its offerings with the needs of their modern enterprise customers.

It preserved its legacy by evolving its identity. Today, IBM is recognized not for what it was, but for what it became.[19]

American Express® (AmEx): From Freight to Finance

AmEx began in the 1850s as a freight forwarding company. Over time, it transitioned into financial services, leveraging its core logistics strengths to build secure, trusted payment systems.

That evolution turned AmEx into a globally recognized financial giant.

Lesson? Your infrastructure might be built for one thing but your future could lie in another.[20]

Chipotle®: Fast Casual, Reimagined

Chipotle was already successful, but it redefined itself by doubling down on its corporate value of food integrity, sourcing local ingredients and emphasizing transparency.

This refocus resonated with a new generation of customers seeking sustainability and trust in their food choices.

The result? Reinforced loyalty, brand differentiation, and renewed relevance.[21]

Play-Doh®: From Wallpaper Cleaner to Childhood Staple

Originally developed in the 1930s to clean wallpaper, Play-Doh found new life when children began using it to shape ornaments.

Recognizing this unexpected market use case, the creators reinvented and rebranded it as a safe modeling clay for children.

That pivot forever changed their trajectory and created a beloved household brand.[22]

Sword Health®: From Digital Health to Virtual Physical Therapy

Sword Health originally focused on digital health. But they saw a more acute need for accessible, personalized, at-home physical therapy.

They shifted their offering to deliver virtual therapy sessions, expanding their reach and impact, especially in a post-pandemic healthcare environment.

Innovation here was about relevance, not reinvention.[23]

Second Order Effects®: From Consulting to Product Innovation

Initially an engineering consultancy, Second Order Effects shifted into creating specialized products in emerging tech, like robotics and AI.

They used their engineering prowess to enter new verticals with high-growth potential.[24]

Able®: From Tech Consultancy to Software Creator

Able began as a tech consulting firm. But by listening deeply to client needs, they transitioned into building custom software solutions designed to streamline operations.

That evolution grew their value—and relevance—in a saturated market.

They didn't wait for reinvention to be forced on them.

They chose it. Before decline became the default.[25]

The Hidden Cost of Doing Nothing

Leaders might think, "We're not really failing. We're just not growing."

But stagnation IS decline—just in disguise.

History is filled with companies who delayed action until it was too late.

They didn't lack ideas. They lacked ***urgency.***

And by the time they realized that standing still was the most dangerous move of all, the window had already closed.

Innovation inertia is invisible—until it's irreversible.

The Cost of Standing Still

Now let's talk about the companies that didn't move fast enough...or maybe not at all.

HHGregg®

Once a go-to for electronics and appliances, HHGregg failed to compete with online retailers and didn't modernize its model. By 2017, it was bankrupt.[26]

Stein Mart®

Known for affordable fashion, Stein Mart never cracked e-commerce. As the retail landscape shifted, it fell behind. It filed for bankruptcy in 2020.[27]

Pier 1 Imports®

Loved for its exotic home goods, Pier 1 couldn't adapt to changing consumer preferences or rising digital competition. The brand collapsed under the weight of high overhead and outdated models.[28]

Thomas Cook®

One of the world's oldest travel agencies, Thomas Cook failed to embrace online booking trends. By 2019, a lack of digital transformation led to total collapse.[29]

Pan Am®

Once the crown jewel of international air travel, Pan Am crumbled due to regulatory shifts and economic missteps. It didn't adapt...and disappeared.[30]

Sharper Image®

Famous for novelty gadgets, Sharper Image failed to evolve with consumer habits and digital retail trends. Bankruptcy followed in 2008.[31]

Gymboree®

A beloved children's brand that didn't keep pace with shifting trends or customer expectations. Bankrupt.[32]

Sears®

It had every opportunity to reinvent itself but didn't. E-commerce could've been its rebirth. Instead, it became its undoing.[33]

Compaq®

A powerhouse in PCs...until it wasn't. Compaq failed to compete on price or evolve on innovation. Eventually absorbed and forgotten.[34]

Yahoo®

At one point, a dominant force in search and digital content.
But mismanagement and missed opportunities (including not buying Google!) led to irrelevance.[35]

RadioShack®

Didn't modernize. Didn't digitize. Didn't survive.[36]

BlackBerry®

Once a leader in smartphones, until it refused to let go of the keyboard. Innovation moved on. BlackBerry didn't.[37] (More on BlackBerry later.)

Sports Authority®

Failed to adapt to digital commerce or adopt competitive pricing. Closed in 2016.[38]

These companies didn't just lose market share. They lost relevance.

And relevance—corporately and individually—is what keeps you in the game.

So how do the approaches of the Innovative Thinkers and the Historical Footnotes differ?

Innovators vs. Footnotes: A Strategic Comparison

Innovative Thinkers	Historical Footnotes
Embraced change before they were forced to	Resisted changed–even when the writing was on the wall
Leveraged existing assets, capabilities, and insights	Over-relied on past successes and legacy thinking
Stayed close to their customers and evolving needs	Misunderstood or ignored changing customer preferences
Acted decisively while others hesitated	Delayed action until it was too late
Reimagined offerings to align with emerging market dynamics	Clung to outdated business models despite environmental shifts
Used agility to adapt to technological advancements	Failed to recognize or invest in relevant technologies
Led cultural shifts internally to support innovation	Maintained rigid organizational structures that stifled adaptability
Saw maturity as a launchpad for reinvention	Saw maturity as as reason to protect the *status quo*
Invested in continuous learning and market listening	Operated from assumptions rather than current insight
Viewed innovation as a core leadership responsibility	Treated innovation as a side project or departmental function

Last Thoughts: The Real Divide

The difference between the success stories and the cautionary tales isn't luck.

It's leadership.

The innovators embraced change before they were forced to. They leveraged what they already had. They stayed close to their customers. They acted when others hesitated.

This is the InnoMagination imperative.

The whole point of InnoMagination is this:

> **You don't need to build something new. You need to see what you already have—differently.**

The companies that thrive in today's market understand that.

The ones that don't? They become footnotes.

Reflection Prompts for Leaders

Use these prompts to turn insight into action:

- Are we building a future? Or protecting a past?
- What assumptions are we making about our product, market, or model that need to be challenged?
- Do we have the courage to pivot before we're forced to?
- Which story in this chapter felt uncomfortably familiar? Why?
- What internal strengths are we under-leveraging right now?

Six

Rethinking Innovation with MPI & the InnoMagination Framework

"Innovation is taking two things that already exist and putting them together in a new way."

— Tom Freston

Chapter Objective: *Introduce the concept of Marketing Powered Innovation and the **InnoMagination™** Framework as a structured, cross-functional approach to unlocking growth by reimagining existing assets through the strategic lens of Marketing + Consulting + Innovation.*

When most leaders think "innovation," they instinctively picture groundbreaking technologies, flashy product launches, or entirely new inventions. But that's a dangerously narrow view.

There's an enormous problem with that narrative. It's incomplete. Worse, it's misleading.

Innovation isn't limited to what you invent next. It's also about how you leverage what you already have, in ways your customers never imagined possible.

Innovation doesn't always come from the R&D lab.

Sometimes, it comes straight from Marketing.

The Rise of Marketing Powered Innovation

This is where Marketing Powered Innovation (MPI) comes in.

MPI isn't marketing (the function or the verb) as usual. It's not what is often viewed outside the function as 'branding fluff' or even post-launch promotion. It's Marketing (the Department and its people) as a strategic, revenue-driving force that uncovers untapped growth inside your existing products, services, and capabilities.

It's how you outmaneuver the competition without blowing up your roadmap...or your budget.

And given today's volatile, resource-constrained, high-pressure environment, it's exactly what you need.

So What Exactly Is It?

Marketing Powered Innovation (MPI) is a strategic approach that positions Marketing as a ***catalyst*** *of innovation, leveraging deep market and customer insight, competitive intelligence, and strategic business understanding to rapidly uncover and execute unseen and unmet market opportunities. Rather than building from scratch, MPI strategically* ***reimagines existing assets, capabilities, and core organizational strengths*** *into profitable new value. It transforms Marketing into a proactive driver of growth and cross-functional alignment.*

It is built upon the foundation of:

- Market and customer insight
- Competitive intelligence
- Brand strategy
- Go-To-Market execution

MPI is based on one of the many flavors of Innovation, what practitioners call ***Recombinant Innovation***[39]. Its goal is to create new value by reimagining the assets, insights, and capabilities you already have. Not building from scratch. ***Reimagining from strength.***

The Four Pillars of Marketing Powered Innovation

1. Marketing as the Tip of the Spear

Marketing is often closer to the pulse of the market than any other function, save Sales. And as Tony Robbins famously says, "proximity is power". MPI positions the Marketing team as the first to see what's changing...and the first to act on it.

Marketing becomes the vanguard of strategic innovation, identifying untapped value within existing assets and offerings and getting it to market fast.

2. Marketing as a Profit Center

MPI flips the script on the old perception of Marketing as a cost center. Instead, it reframes Marketing as a profit center, a driver of new revenue and Return on Marketing Investment (ROMI) through rapid insight-to-market execution.

Instead of long R&D cycles, MPI delivers speed, clarity, and relevance—getting new value into the hands of customers while your competitors are still whiteboarding.

3. Marketing as a Growth Leader

MPI is a leadership play that elevates the CMO and the Marketing team to the role of Growth Architects. These are people who don't just tell the story, but actually shape business strategy.

This is where GTM becomes innovation with teeth. It's where visibility turns into influence. It's where the Marketing function earns its seat at the Growth table...and keeps it.

4. Innovation is for Everyone

MPI isn't a land grab where Marketing plots to take over Innovation or Product. Rather, it's Marketing leading cross-functional orchestration and collaboration for the good of the entire organization.

Marketing brings insights. Product brings technical depth. Sales and Customer Service (or Success) brings customer intimacy. Together, they move as one. MPI creates the connective tissue that makes innovation scalable, aligned, and deeply customer-centered.

Standing on the Shoulders of Giants: An Evolving Legacy of Marketing Innovation

Marketing Powered Innovation isn't a new idea pulled from thin air. It's a strategic evolution, one that builds on the foundational work of innovation visionaries who saw where the world was headed long before most organizations did.

Peter Drucker gave us the foundational lens:

- Innovation is a systematic process focused on creating customer value.

- He made it clear that innovation wasn't about inspiration. It was about disciplined execution. He also famously said business has only two functions: marketing and innovation.[40] MPI is the bridge that connects both.

Clayton Christensen offered the disruption playbook:

- Disruption happens when companies ignore emerging needs in favor of protecting the *status quo*.

- His work showed how markets can be reshaped by innovators who prioritize relevance over legacy.[41] MPI enables your organization to adopt that mindset, before disruption forces your hand.

George S. Day brought structure to strategy:

- Organizations must be built to be market-driven, not just market-aware.

- He emphasized that the companies that win are the ones that align their internal systems with external insight.[42] MPI further operationalizes that philosophy through cross-functional collaboration and rapid GTM activation.

Marketing Powered Innovation is where all three perspectives converge. It takes Drucker's value-driven systemization, Christensen's disruptive market foresight, and Day's organizational rigor and market-driven approach and brings them to life through the power and engine of the Marketing department, turning insight into impact at-speed.

Marketing Powered Innovation vs. Market-Driven Innovation

Dimension	Marketing Powered Innovation	Market-Driven Innovation
Orientation	Proactive - anticipates and shapes future customer needs	Reactive - responds to current, known customer needs
Marketing's Role	Integrated and leading - Marketing catalyzes innovation from ideation to execution	Supportive - Marketing enters post-ideation to help communicate and promote
Customer Involvement	Co-creative - customers actively shape innovation alongside internal teams	Consultative - customer feedback is collected and analyzed after development
Use of Data & Tech	Deeply data-powered - leverages advanced analytics and AI to guide innovation	Primarily research-based - relies on traditional market research and trends
Market Engagement	Continuous - real-time market input shapes ongoing innovation strategy	Periodic - insights gathered at set intervals or milestones
Innovation Focus	Recombination, reactivation, repositioning, and reimagination of existing assets to derive new value	Often focused on developing net-new solutions to meet current needs
Speed-to-Market	Built for speed - fast iteration and Go-To-Market activation	Slower cycles - longer development and validation timelines
Strategic Alignment	Aligned with organizational Core Essence and GTM from day one	May require retroactive alignment with brand and business strategy

Recombinant Innovation: The Superpower Behind MPI

At the heart of MPI is Recombinant Innovation which takes existing ideas, assets, and capabilities and combines them in new ways to solve different problems or serve new markets.

Recombinant Innovation is efficient, fast, cost-effective, low-risk, and high-reward. It's how smart businesses grow without excessive investment, risk, or internal disruption.

Real-World Examples of Recombinant Innovation in Action

Recombinant Innovation isn't theoretical. Take a look around. It's everywhere when you know how to spot it. Here are two powerful examples that illustrate how this works in practice.

Reese's®: Seeing What Others Miss

Reese's Peanut Butter Cups weren't a lab-born invention. They were a smart combination of two customer favorites. H.B. Reese, responding to a retailer's comment about chocolate peanut butter candy flying off shelves, created something new using what he already had. A roasting equipment glitch gave his peanut butter a standout flavor. During WWII, he focused on just that product, and it worked.

When Hershey® acquired the brand, they amplified it with marketing and distribution. Today, Reese's continues to innovate through consumer-led flavor additions, proving that listening and smart recombination can create lasting value.[43]

Wheeled Luggage: Obvious in Hindsight

Amazingly, we landed on the moon before someone put wheels on a suitcase! The need was apparent—airports were growing (as were distances from curb to gate), and travelers were loaded down and carrying more. After struggling with heavy bags at the airport and observing a worker rolling machinery on a wheeled skid, a luggage executive added wheels to a valise and invented the first wheeled suitcase in 1970.

Later, a pilot refined it into the Rollaboard®, a suitcase with a telescoping handle and two wheels, which became the standard.

Fundamentally, this invention wasn't about new technology, but more simply about paying attention, combining what already existed, and solving a real-world problem better.[44]

MPI and the Three Horizons Framework

Innovation strategists often talk about three "horizons".

- **Horizon 1:** Short-term wins (1-2 years). Incremental improvements to existing products and markets. Operational defense of the core business.
- **Horizon 2:** Mid-term plays (2-5 years). Adjacent markets, new use cases, or business model shifts. Expansion.
- **Horizon 3:** Long-term bets (5-12 years). Disruption. Breakthroughs. Transformative, Blue Ocean Strategy-type moves.

MPI is your go-to that overlaps Horizons 1 and 2; you could think of it as 'Horizon 1.5' but I'm calling it 'The Middle Ground'. It helps you move quickly, stay relevant, and generate ROI while your Horizon 3 innovation engine works in parallel. They're all complementary.

InnoMagination is the ideal framework to execute MPI across 'the Middle Ground' of 6-24 months. It gives you the steps, the strategy, and the speed (upfront and early in the process) to find and activate growth from what you already own.

What Makes *InnoMagination*™ Different

Most innovation frameworks fall into one of three traps:

1. They stay stuck in theory.
2. They focus too narrowly on product development.
3. Or they inspire big ideas, then leave you with no clear way to act on them.

InnoMagination breaks that cycle.

This isn't a brainstorming exercise. It's not a Post-It-Notes -on-the-whiteboard-party. And it's definitely not another brand refresh disguised as a growth plan.

InnoMagination is a full-cycle innovation methodology built for CMOs and Marketing leaders who are ready to lead the way.

It gives you a clear, repeatable process to identify latent value, align cross-functional teams, and drive market-ready outcomes—fast.

It's grounded in the assets you already have, wired for speed, and designed to move across functions, not around them.

Where other frameworks may leave you at the insight phase, ***InnoMagination*** carries you all the way to a validated business case and a clear Go-To-Market strategy that's positioned to win.

It's strategy you can sell.
Innovation you can lead.
Growth you can prove.
That's the difference.

The Intersection of Three Disciplines

Marketing Powered Innovation and the ***InnoMagination*** methodology aren't simply advocating marketing as usual. They strategically integrate some of the most powerful aspects of Marketing, Management

Consulting, and Innovation into one cohesive, repeatable framework.

Marketing: Deep Customer Insight & Strategic Storytelling
Marketing is far more than branding, lead generation, or promotional exercises. The greatest strength of Marketing is its ability to deeply understand customer needs, behaviors, and emotions, and then strategically craft stories and experiences that resonate profoundly at a human level.

Great marketing begins with listening—carefully, consistently, and creatively—to what your customers say, and often more importantly, what they *don't* say. It transforms insights into meaningful differentiation, translating clarity directly into revenue. Marketing, when done strategically, is the ultimate driver of demand, alignment, and growth.

Management Consulting: Structured Analysis & Clear Decision-Making
Management Consulting brings structured thinking, rigorous analysis, and clear decision-making processes to complex organizational challenges. Skilled consultants excel at dissecting ambiguous problems into clear, actionable insights. They build frameworks, models, and methodologies executives trust.

Management Consulting demands clarity, credibility, and measurable impact which is exactly what's needed to move ***InnoMagination*** from exciting ideas to executable business cases.

Innovation: Bold Creativity & Rapid Experimentation
Innovation thrives on bold thinking, creative problem-solving, and rapid experimentation. It demands curiosity, courage, and comfort with uncertainty. Innovation is inherently agile, testing assumptions, learning

fast, iterating quickly, and adapting continuously.

Innovation transforms challenges into opportunities, constraints into creativity, and legacy systems into future-ready engines of growth.

Transformational Change by Uniting Three Disciplines and One Powerful Methodology

Individually, each of these three disciplines—Marketing, Management Consulting, and Innovation—is already powerful. But intentionally combined, these disciplines become transformative:

- Marketing ensures deep customer understanding and compelling positioning.
- Management Consulting creates rigor, clarity, and measurable impact.
- Innovation fosters creativity, agility, and rapid adaptation.

MPI and ***InnoMagination*** deliberately sit at this powerful intersection, integrating the strategic customer insights of Marketing, the rigorous analysis and structured clarity of Management Consulting, and the rapid experimentation and bold creativity of Innovation.

This is why this approach is uniquely effective: It is precisely *because* it is not just Innovation, not just Marketing, and not just Consulting that it is so impactful. It's the strategic, systematic synthesis of all three that unlocks extraordinary results and sustainable growth.

If you're experienced in one of these disciplines, you'll recognize familiar tools and approaches, but you'll also discover new perspectives, methods, and frameworks from the other two disciplines, expanding your toolkit and sharpening your strategic thinking.

MPI and ***InnoMagination*** enable innovation that's strategically rigorous, market-driven, creatively agile, and powerfully profitable.

This is the confluence of possibility, practicality, and profitability.

What sets *InnoMagination* apart from other approaches?

1. Core Essence Discovery

InnoMagination starts by helping you rediscover what makes your organization unique: your values, your purpose, your positioning, and more. This articulation anchors everything that follows, ensuring innovation efforts align with who you are and where you're going. This is not just the typical brand exercise—it includes brand, yes, but it delves deeper.

2. Asset Identification

Next, we surface the under-leveraged products, capabilities, and strengths already sitting inside your organization. You don't need to invent from scratch. You need to see your existing assets through a new lens.

3. Reuse of Existing Assets

This step unlocks the hidden potential within your current offerings. By reimagining existing products and capabilities, you can quickly pivot and adapt to new market demands with minimal risk and investment.

4. Unmet Market Need Analysis

Then we layer in real-world insight: what customers want, where the market is shifting, and where unmet demand lives. This is where opportunity meets readiness.

From Insight to Execution—Without the Gaps

Unlike many frameworks that stop at developing strategy, ***InnoMagination*** connects the dots between ideation and execution. It's built to move your team from internal discovery to external impact through a structured, time-bound process that drives clarity, momentum, and
alignment.

Most organizations can complete developing the full ***InnoMagination*** roadmap in 4 to 12 weeks or less, with tangible deliverables in hand:

- A validated opportunity with ROI estimates
- A clear Go-To-Market path
- An executive-facing business case

It's fast, focused, and built to work with the resources you already have.

The ***InnoMagination*** framework gives you more than a plan.

It gives you a system for seeing differently, thinking strategically, and executing with confidence.

That's the difference. And that's the opportunity.

What the Latest Research Says

McKinsey's 2024 research points out:

> *"Organizations can raise revenues by enhancing the benefits of current offerings and providing new and innovative customer experiences."*

They also stress that:

> ***"Eighty percent of the value creation achieved by the world's most successful growth companies comes from their core business—principally, unlocking new revenues from existing customers."*** [45]

Sound familiar? That's pretty much MPI in a nutshell.
You don't need to reinvent the wheel. You just need to make the wheels you already have spin smoother, faster, and further.

Where the Untapped Potential Lives
Think of MPI as a lens that reveals value you've been walking past.

It helps you uncover:

- **New markets** to reposition or offerings to repackage for different customer segments.
- **Strategic tweaks** for minor enhancements with outsized customer impact.
- **Business model adjustments** like subscription models, bundling, tiered pricing, etc.
- **Partnership strategies** to develop external collaborations to amplify reach and capability.

These aren't pipe dreams. They're practical moves that drive growth without draining resources.

Last Thoughts: Innovation *InnoMagined*

Practically speaking, the next breakthrough inside your business probably isn't a brand-new product.

It's a sharper way of seeing what you already have and turning that into something more.

Marketing Powered Innovation is how you align your teams, activate your assets, and accelerate growth without blowing up your roadmap or your core business.

InnoMagination is the step-by-step, repeatable process that makes that possible.

It's the framework built to operationalize MPI, turning insight into action, and potential into performance.

And it's exactly what your team is capable of...starting now.

Reflection Prompts for Leaders

Use these prompts to turn insight into action:

- Are we overlooking ***InnoMagination*** opportunities hiding in plain sight?
- Is our Marketing team positioned to drive ***InnoMagination*** or just promote it?
- Are we using our existing assets to their full potential?
- Where are we missing the chance to recombine what we already have for new value?

SEVEN

7 CORE PRINCIPLES OF INNOMAGINATION: THE ART OF REIMAGINING

"Discovery consists of seeing what everybody has seen and thinking what nobody has thought."

— Albert Szent-Györgyi

Chapter Objective: *Introduce the seven core principles of the* ***InnoMagination™*** *framework, showing how maturing organizations can drive faster, lower-risk innovation by reimagining existing assets through a structured, customer-centered process.*

As a CMO or Growth leader, you already know the pressure: deliver growth (quarter after quarter after quarter *ad infinitum…*), keep customers and stakeholders happy, stay relevant…and do it all within budget.

The problem? Most innovation frameworks are built around new product development which entail long timelines, high risk, and heavy CapEx investment. And for many maturing organizations, that model just isn't compatible with the organization's expectations for rapid return without the risk and without spending a lot of money to get it.

Fortunately, ***InnoMagination*** offers a different path. It's targeted for the Middle Ground timeframe of 6-24 months, which enables you to deliver results quickly.

Instead of betting the future on what you haven't built yet, ***InnoMagination*** helps you unleash revenue, relevance, and reach by reimagining what's already in your portfolio. These are products and capabilities that have been proven to work and that you can deliver. It's a smarter way to innovate: faster, de-risked, and rooted in the assets, insights, and capabilities you already have.

Here's how it works.

The 7 Principles That Power *InnoMagination*

These are the seven core principles that make ***InnoMagination*** both strategic and actionable. Together, they form a solid, directional scaffold that enables companies to grow from within.

1. Harnessing Latent Assets

This is where it starts...by looking inward.

Instead of defaulting to net-new products, the framework challenges leaders to surface under-utilized products, services, and capabilities—and put them to work in new ways. That might mean repurposing a feature for a new use case, repositioning an existing offer for a different segment, or combining assets in a way that offers fresh value.

It's turning what you already have into what the market wants **now or will want very soon**.

For example, a software company may realize that a lightly used feature in its enterprise suite could be spun off as a much needed standalone solution for small businesses, getting that capability to market faster and cheaper than building something from scratch.

The result? Lower risk. Higher speed. Faster returns.

2. Market-Driven Insights

Before you innovate, you need to listen.

This principle requires getting grounded in market reality: what your customers care about, how their needs are shifting, and where competitors are falling short. It's critical you stop any guessing and gain evidence-based clarity.

This is where you use real data insights to validate demand, shape direction, and guide every next step.

Let's say you have a strong product line, but your customers are evolving toward a different value set, like sustainability or automation. That insight gives you a chance to reposition, repackage, or reframe your messaging to meet the moment.

3. Product Repositioning

Once you know what the market wants, you can reframe what you already offer.

Repositioning is a powerful lever. It allows you to shift perception, reach new audiences, and reintroduce existing offerings in ways that feel new and relevant.

You might find that a product built for one vertical (for example Financial

Services) is a perfect fit for another (Public Sector). Or that with a slight tweak in messaging, packaging, or delivery, a legacy product becomes the perfect solution for an emerging market.

Example: A consumer electronics company cross-markets a best-selling tablet as a tool for remote work, not just entertainment. Same product. New context. Expanded relevance.

4. Cross-Functional Collaboration
InnoMagination doesn't live in one department. It flourishes in the spaces across and between business 'kingdoms'.

This principle breaks down silos and gets your smartest people in the same room—Marketing, Sales, Customer Success, Product, Ops. When these teams collaborate early, ***InnoMagination*** becomes more grounded, more executable, and more aligned.

The magic happens when different and diverse perspectives collide and Spark to solve the same problem.

5. Accelerated Time-to-Market
Speed matters (obviously!). ***InnoMagination*** leverages what you already have, enabling you to move faster than traditional R&D-led innovation. You're not building from zero. You're experimenting, iterating, repositioning, and activating with clarity and confidence.

This principle empowers you to seize market moments before your competitors do. It also means your Go-To-Market team isn't waiting on Product to do their thing then hand it off to be launched. They're helping shape it from the beginning.

6. Customer-Centric Solutions

At the center of all this is the customer. This principle ensures that your ***InnoMagination*** efforts are anchored in real customer needs—not internal assumptions. That means listening deeply, testing early, and staying flexible enough to adapt as feedback comes in.

A company that actively listens to its customers can spot new use cases, remove friction, and improve retention, all without having to invent something new.

7. Structured Process

This isn't a brainstorming session. It's a system.

InnoMagination is a guided, repeatable process—typically run over 4 to 12 weeks—that moves your team from insight to execution through clear stages:

- Audit your current products, services, and capabilities
- Analyze market shifts, customer needs, and competitive gaps
- Collaborate across functions to identify and prioritize opportunities
- Obtain executive buy-in and activate with a sharp, cross-functional Go-To-Market plan
- Validate quickly and cost-effectively

The ***InnoMagination*** process turns innovation from an abstract goal into an executable path.

The Path to Sustainable Growth
You don't always need something new to grow.

You just need to look at what you already have with a sharper lens, a tighter strategy, and a clear process.

InnoMagination gives you that lens. It gives you the method. And it gives you the confidence to act in a fast and focused way.

Your takeaway is simple. **Rapidly accessible, sustainable growth doesn't begin with invention. It begins with reimagination.**

By applying the ***InnoMagination*** framework, you can turn existing products and capabilities into new relevance, new revenue, and renewed momentum, without waiting for the next big thing to come from your R&D Department.

Because it's likely already in your hands, waiting to be *InnoMagined.*

This is the art—and the discipline—of ***InnoMagination***.

It's how organizations stay relevant, resilient, and ready to lead.

Reflection Prompts for Leaders

Use these prompts to turn insight into action:

- Where are we under-utilizing assets that could be repositioned?
- Are our innovation efforts aligned with what the market actually wants right now?
- How cross-functional is our current innovation process? Where can we improve it?
- Are we moving as fast as we could... or are we waiting for perfection?
- What's one product we could reframe or repurpose this quarter?

EIGHT

INNOMAGINATION VS. TRADITIONAL INNOVATION: A PARADIGM SHIFT

"Don't follow the crowd. Let the crowd follow you."

— Attributed to Margaret Thatcher

Chapter Objective: *Redefine innovation by contrasting traditional approaches with the* ***InnoMagination™*** *model, highlighting how Marketing Powered Innovation unlocks faster, lower-risk growth by reimagining existing assets through a cross-functional, customer-led lens.*

You already know this: Innovation is your lifeline to sustained growth, market leadership, and customer loyalty. But when we talk about "innovation," we often fall into traps, assuming it means massive investments, high-risk bets, and long, uncertain timelines. There's an underlying bias against anything that could be considered "incremental"...as if incremental is a bad word!

This bias can block real progress, keeping you stuck in inertia, waiting for "perfect" conditions that never arrive.

It's time to shift your thinking. To do something different.

The simple beauty of *InnoMagination* is that it doesn't have to mean invention. And it usually doesn't mean massive disruption.

InnoMagination can be as elegantly powerful as seeing your own products, people, and processes through a fresh lens.

Traditional Innovation: Two Extremes, One Critical Gap

There are many types of traditional innovation and they generally fall into one of two buckets:

- **Long-term breakthroughs:** Big bets. Industry-shifting products involving large investments in time, talent, and capital. These can change the world, but they're also usually risky, costly, and slow.

- **Short-term efficiencies:** Small-scale improvements, operational tweaks, and cost-cutting. These are safer bets but are rarely transformative.

The problem is that between these two extremes lies a massive, overlooked opportunity to reinvent what's already in your hands. As we previously discussed, this short-to-mid-range 'Middle Ground' gap (6 to 24 months out or less) often goes ignored, even though it's exactly where your most immediate growth opportunities exist.

InnoMagination: Innovation in the Middle Ground

InnoMagination fills that gap, combining strategic thinking, market insights, and rapid execution to innovate where it counts most, leveraging your existing products, services, and capabilities.

It's not reinventing the wheel. It's seeing clearly, thinking creatively, and acting strategically to **innovate by reimagining what you already have**.

Marketing as Your Catalyst: The Power of MPI

Here's what sets the ***InnoMagination*** approach to innovation apart: ***Marketing Powered* Innovation (MPI)**.

MPI shifts ***InnoMagination*** from isolated R&D labs or dedicated innovation teams into the hands of your Marketing team. This is a group that's already deeply connected to market trends, customer insights, competitive landscapes, and creative thinking.

Marketing becomes the catalyst, using tools you already have—analytics, competitive research, customer feedback—to guide rapid, targeted ***InnoMagination*** development, experiments, and execution. ***InnoMagination*** is democratized innovation. You don't need big budgets or specialized innovation teams. You just need to SEE differently, SPARK collaboration, and DO more with what's already there.

Overcoming Resource Constraints: How to Innovate Within Your Means

Traditional innovation demands resources many organizations just can't spare. MPI provides another, easily accessible option. It helps you innovate within existing budgets, teams, and timelines, allowing even resource-constrained organizations to compete effectively.

You don't need massive investments. You need strategic realignment. Instead of chasing costly new inventions, you create growth by repositioning what you already offer, targeting new markets, and reimagining existing solutions.

Leveraging Existing Resources: SEE What You Already Have

InnoMagination doesn't require new infrastructure or massive retooling. With ***InnoMagination***, your existing production processes, capabilities, and knowledge become launchpads for growth. The entire point is to determine what has already worked, what you are already capable of delivering, without having to spend a lot of time or money or take on much risk.

Consider how tweaking an existing product feature can quickly solve a new customer pain point. Or how repositioning a legacy product for an emerging trend can open entirely new revenue streams.

For example, if you are a Software-as-a-Service company targeting a particular user, could you make the fairly simple changes to the permissions on the software to create another user type so that you could sell adjacent audiences within the same enterprise customer? This would take minimal time or investment, could be executed through your Marketing engine, and enable you to expand within existing accounts while making your solution stickier with a higher propensity for renewal.

You reduce risk, accelerate timelines, and amplify ROI, simply by doing more with what you already have.

Sustainability as a Core Principle: DO More with Less

Sustainability isn't a buzzword. Well, ok, it IS, but it is also a very real strategic imperative. And MPI naturally aligns with sustainability because it repurposes assets you already possess.

Take Nerds® candy, for instance. Originally a waste byproduct of another candy's manufacturing process, smart marketing turned these leftover sugar bits into a beloved treat. The company didn't discard the waste; they just reimagined and adopted creative packaging specifically designed for their middle school-aged target market to make it a runaway favorite. Sustainability met profitability.

The brand has since spun off additional product lines and as of 2024, creates $700 million in annual revenue. Ironically, the candy declined for many years prior, bringing in only $40 million per year. The company was able to resurrect the brand by marrying the best of two products—the original Nerds plus Nerds Gummy Rope®—to create a next-generation product that satisfies specific desires of their market.[46]

InnoMagination resonates with environmentally conscious consumers. It builds brand loyalty, enhances reputation, and creates real, lasting value.

Dual Focus: Revenue Growth and Customer Centricity

InnoMagination thrives on customer-centric insights. By staying close to customer needs and market shifts, you ensure your innovations aren't just clever. They're relevant, resonant, and revenue-generating.

Your customers tell you exactly what they want. MPI gives you the agility to respond...fast.

Cross-Functional Collaboration: SPARK New Ideas Together

InnoMagination doesn't happen in silos. It happens when diverse teams, like Marketing, Sales, Product, and Customer Success, collaborate to SPARK new opportunities and DO something about them.

InnoMagination encourages teams to brainstorm, prototype, experiment, and iterate together. The result? Richer ideas, faster buy-in, and quicker execution.

Accelerated Time-to-Market: DO It Faster

Traditional innovation can mean years of development. ***InnoMagination*** can move quickly, within 6 to 24 months (or even less) from insight to market to ROI.

This speed lets you capitalize on emerging trends before competitors even notice. It helps you respond swiftly, seize opportunities, and seize market leadership.

Building Agility into Your Culture: SEE, SPARK, DO. Repeat.

InnoMagination isn't just a method; it's a mindset. By continually reimagining your current offerings, you build an agile culture, ready to pivot, experiment, and adapt.

InnoMagination becomes a habit, not a one-time event. Your team learns to SEE opportunities everywhere, SPARK ideas and collaboration quickly, and DO what matters most, now.

Last Thoughts: Augment Your Innovation Strategy with *InnoMagination*

Traditional innovation still matters, but it's no longer enough. You can no longer do what you have historically done. You need a fresh approach. An approach that leverages existing assets, minimizes risk, and moves swiftly.

InnoMagination is that approach. It's how you SEE differently, SPARK growth quickly, and DO what your competitors can't.

Marketing leaders, your imperative is absolutely clear. Don't wait for perfect conditions. Don't just rely solely on costly, slow-moving, traditional innovation methods. Instead, **SEE** what's already in your hands, **SPARK** new possibilities, and **DO** the work to make it happen.

InnoMagination is your strategic unlock. You are the linchpin at the intersection of customer insight, brand storytelling, and market opportunity. But too often, Marketing is treated as a support function instead of a strategic driver of innovation.

InnoMagination changes the paradigm. It positions Marketing as ***the*** catalyst for growth—bringing together data, creativity, and cross-functional collaboration to reimagine existing offerings and accelerate time to market.

With MPI, you don't have to wait on Product or R&D to bring you a product to take to market. Now YOU lead the charge. You already have the insights; you can own the ***InnoMagination*** agenda.

This is your opportunity to move from messenger to maker. To drive growth not just through campaigns, but through transformation.

This is your growth lever hiding in plain sight. Your job is to drive sustainable, scalable growth and innovation. Unfortunately, in today's chaotic market, traditional growth levers (hiring, expansion, net-new product development) are slow, expensive, and increasingly risky.

InnoMagination gives you a smarter path. This is your call to release the untapped revenue from what you already have. To reposition legacy offerings, repackage features for new markets, and rethink how your assets do and could create value going forward.

This isn't just squeezing more from the same. It's activating the dormant potential that's already built, tested, and trusted. ***InnoMagination*** is your bridge between operational efficiency and exponential growth. It gives you speed, clarity, and a repeatable path to outcomes that matter.

This is the paradigm shift your growth strategy needs. And the future of your organization depends on it.

Reflection Prompts for Leaders

Use these prompts to turn insight into action:

- Are we overlooking mid-range ***InnoMagination*** opportunities that leverage our existing assets?
- Is our Marketing team empowered to drive proactive ***InnoMagination***, or are they stuck promoting in the traditional, after-the-fact Marketing model?
- How can we better collaborate across functions to accelerate ***InnoMagination***?
- Are we moving fast enough to capture market opportunities, or are we waiting for "perfect"?
- What's one product, service, or capability we can reposition this quarter to SPARK new growth?

NINE

THE INNOMAGINATION PLAYBOOK

> ***"Innovation is not the product of logical thought, although the result is tied to logical structure."***
>
> ***— Albert Einstein***

The *InnoMagination™* Process: An Overview

InnoMagination is a structured, repeatable approach to innovation that leverages your existing assets, uncovers hidden market opportunities, and clearly maps a path from insight to execution, in a de-risked manner with low or no capital expenditure.

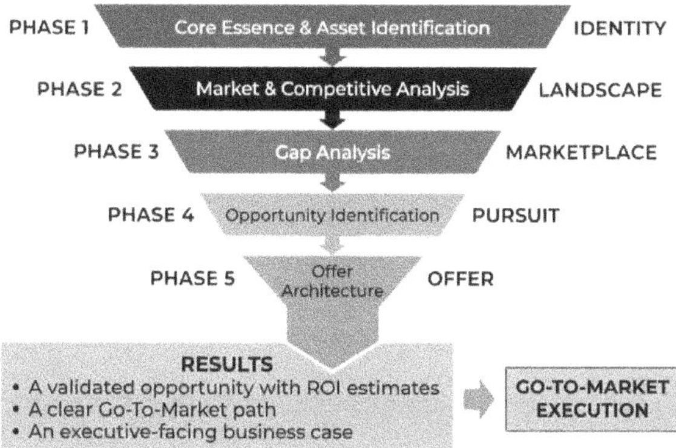

This chapter is the playbook for the whole methodology. We have a lot to cover, but before we get into the detail, I want to give you a bit of an overview of the sections we'll go over:

- Phase 1: IDENTITY
  - Discovering Your Core Essence—The Foundation for *InnoMagination*
  - The Asset Inventory Audit—SEE Clearly What's Already There

- Phase 2: LANDSCAPE
  - Industry Insights: Fertile Grounds for Leveraging Existing Assets
  - Data-Driven Dreaming: The Role of Analytics in *InnoMagination*

- Phase 3: MARKETPLACE
  - The Voice of the Customer: Feedback as Fuel for *InnoMagination*
  - Scenarios, Market Gaps & Unmet Needs! Oh My!

- Phase 4: PURSUIT
  - Evaluating Your *InnoMagination* Opportunities

- Phase 5: OFFER
  - Collaboration in Action: Cross-Functional Teams & Change Management
  - Aligning InnoMagination with Vision: Ensuring Strategic Coherence
  - Metrics of Success: Measuring *InnoMagination* Effectively
  - Building An Effective Business Case

The Five Phases of ***InnoMagination*** are:

Phase 1: IDENTITY – Core Essence & Asset Identification
We start by clarifying your organization's *Core Essence*—your values, purpose, positioning, etc.—and identifying under-leveraged assets already within your business. This foundational clarity helps anchor your ***InnoMagination*** efforts in authenticity and strategic coherence.

Phase 2: LANDSCAPE – Market & Competitive Analysis
Next, we explore the external landscape, analyzing market trends, competitive dynamics, and industry shifts. Here, we look outward, identifying fertile grounds where your existing assets can thrive in new or emerging contexts.

Phase 3: MARKETPLACE – Gap Analysis
In the Marketplace phase, we identify market gaps and unmet customer needs. By systematically mapping your internal assets against external opportunities, we pinpoint precisely where you can create differentiated and high-value offerings your competitors have overlooked.

Phase 4: PURSUIT – Opportunity Identification
In Pursuit, we strategically evaluate and prioritize the identified opportunities. This step ensures you focus resources on the most strategically aligned, high-impact initiative, reducing risk while maximizing return.

Phase 5: OFFER – Offer Architecture

Finally, we architect a compelling, market-ready offer. Cross-functional collaboration ensures internal alignment, while a clear and executive-ready business case outlines expected ROI, market positioning, and the specific Go-To-Market path forward.

What's the Outcome?

- A validated ***InnoMagination*** opportunity with clear ROI estimates
- A concrete, actionable Go-To-Market roadmap
- An executive-ready business case that accelerates internal buy-in and execution

Phase 1: IDENTITY
Identifying Innovative Opportunities: Which Products Hold Potential?

"Vision is the art of seeing what is invisible to others."

—Jonathan Swift

Section Objective: *Guide leaders through the first step of the* ***InnoMagination*** *process by identifying high-potential products within their existing portfolio, using Core Essence discovery, asset audits, and strategic alignment to uncover overlooked opportunities for* ***InnoMagination****.*

You know this already...Innovation is essential for growth and staying competitive. Unfortunately, maturing companies often overlook a tragic irony: your greatest opportunities might just be hidden within your existing products and services. While you're busy chasing shiny new ideas, you're leaving diamonds buried in your own backyard.

It's easy to assume older products have fully exhausted their market potential. But this complacency blinds you to opportunities for repositioning or repurposing. Many iconic brands have successfully reinvented products for new markets, achieving renewed relevance. Challenge the assumption that existing products are tapped out. Look again, think creatively, and see new possibilities emerge.

Consider baking soda. For decades, Arm & Hammer® baking soda was known as a simple baking ingredient, sitting quietly in pantries across America. Its market seemed mature, fully saturated, and tapped out. Yet, by repositioning this humble household staple into new categories—as a refrigerator deodorizer, toothpaste additive, carpet freshener, laundry booster, and more—Arm & Hammer unlocked entirely new revenue streams and refreshed its brand relevance. [47]

They didn't reinvent the product; they simply connected with how customers were already using it in some cases and in other cases, reimagined how it could be used, marketed, and valued. It's time to shift your mindset. Let's SEE what you might be overlooking, SPARK a movement in your organization, then DO something powerful with it.

STEP 1: Discovering Your *Core Essence*—The Foundation for *InnoMagination*

To SEE clearly which products hold the most potential, start by uncovering your organization's ***Core Essence***. Like an individual's fingerprint, this powerful blend of five foundational elements is unique and distinguishes you from all the other organizations in the world. The elements—*organizational personality, mission, corporate values, brand promise, and brand perception*—mesh together to serve as your compass, guiding your ***InnoMagination*** decisions and illuminating hidden opportunities.

Uncover Your Organizational Personality

Just like a person, your organization has its own unique personality...the beliefs, behaviors, and energy that shape interactions internally and externally.

Begin discovery by:

- Conducting internal surveys to capture employee perspectives
- Hosting cross-departmental focus groups for richer insights
- Analyzing external perceptions through customer feedback and social listening

Refine Your Mission Statement

Your mission guides your decisions. You may have had one crafted for many years but is it still relevant? Does it continue to inspire your team and resonate with your customers?

Verify your mission statement by:

- Facilitating strategic workshops to review and refine your mission
- Drafting multiple versions to test for clarity and inspiration
- Finalizing and communicating a mission statement that motivates everyone toward shared goals

Articulate Your Corporate Values

Values shape culture and decision-making. They must be authentic, clear, and consistently applied.

Confirm your values by:

- Holding leadership alignment sessions to clearly define or refine your values

- Engaging employees to build ownership and commitment
- Integrating values into daily practices, from hiring to customer interactions

Consider Your Brand Promise

Your brand promise sets customer expectations. Are you consistently delivering on it?

Revisit your brand promise by:

- Evaluating customer feedback regularly
- Ensuring alignment between your promise and actual experiences
- Performing consistency checks in all marketing and customer communications

Understand Your Brand Perception

How the market perceives your brand might differ from your intentions. Discovering and bridging this gap is essential.

Check your alignment by:

- Conducting market research and social media analysis to assess perception
- Implementing strategies to align perception with your intended brand promise

Once you've articulated your *Core Essence*, compile it into a clear, shareable internal profile. You'll use this profile later in the *Asset Category Matrix* exercise to strategically evaluate each product's alignment and potential.

Warning! Do NOT skip this step! It is the basis of all the other steps in the InnoMagination process.

STEP 2: The Asset Inventory Audit—SEE Clearly What's Already There

An *Asset Inventory Audit* is like deep spring cleaning for your business. It's not just tidying up. This is uncovering hidden gems and seeing fresh opportunities in what you already own.

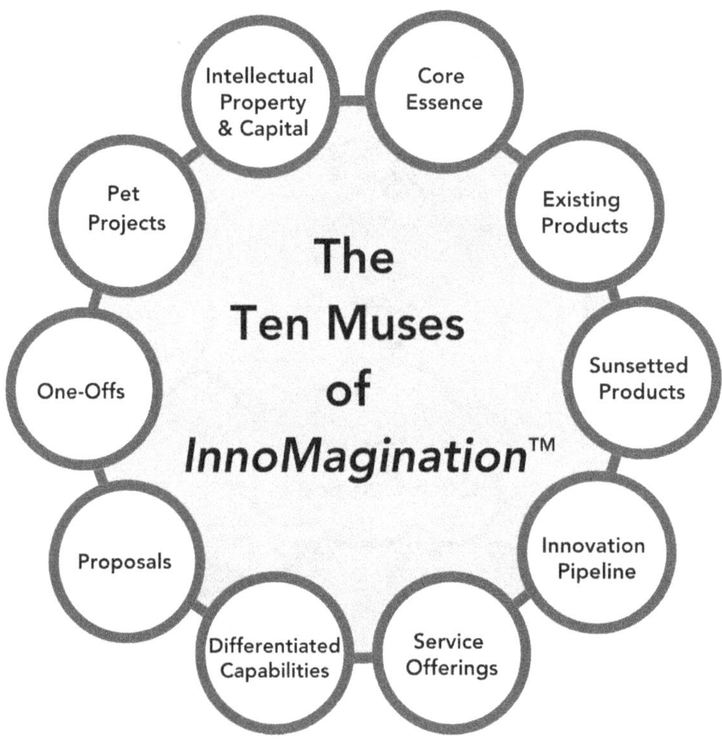

To structure your audit, start by exploring ***"The Ten Muses of InnoMagination"***. These are products, services, and capabilities within your business that can serve as sources of inspiration to you. Send out a data call throughout the organization (a simple Google Form will do) and ask specifically for team members to list everything they can think of in the following categories:

1. ***Core Essence Profile*:** The foundation you've just defined. Your 'fingerprint' is an asset!

2. **Existing Products:** Identify overlooked potential for enhancement or repositioning.

3. **Sunsetted Products:** Could these discontinued offerings find new life in new markets?

4. **Products in the Pipeline:** Analyze potential markets, partnerships, or applications. Make sure to look across divisions.

5. **Intellectual Property (IP) or Intellectual Capital (IC):** Discover new ways to repurpose or perhaps partner or license patents, brands, trademarks, methods, processes, databases, customer relationships, or human capital.

6. **Service Offerings:** Explore ways custom services could scale to broader audiences.

7. **Proposed Products & Services:** Revisit ideas that were previously proposed but not sold.

8. **One-Offs:** Commercialize isolated solutions into scalable offerings.

9. **Differentiated Capabilities:** Leverage internal strengths (like exceptional customer service or partner relationships) into consultative offerings or bundles.

10. **Secret or Pet Projects:** Surface and evaluate innovative side-projects within the organization.

Embrace this audit process as a systematic exploration. SEE what's overlooked. SPARK fresh ideas. DO the work to reveal new opportunities.

Tip: Revisit this audit every 3-6 months. Record and share across the organization.

STEP 3: The *InnoMagination* Asset Category Matrix—Strategically Aligning Your Portfolio

Finally, use the ***InnoMagination Asset Category Matrix***—a modified version of the classic BCG matrix—to categorize your assets strategically. Unlike traditional market-focused matrices, this version emphasizes alignment between your *Core Essence* and your ***InnoMagination*** potential, categorizing assets as:

- **Visionaries:** *High impact, high alignment*: Invest aggressively.
- **Explorers:** *High impact, low alignment*: Assess and realign strategically.
- **Guardians:** *Low impact, high alignment*: Stabilize and leverage as ***InnoMagination*** platforms.
- **Niche Creators:** *Low impact, low alignment:* Evaluate carefully and invest sparingly.

Perform this exercise quarterly. This ongoing discipline keeps your portfolio strategically sharp and continuously adaptive.

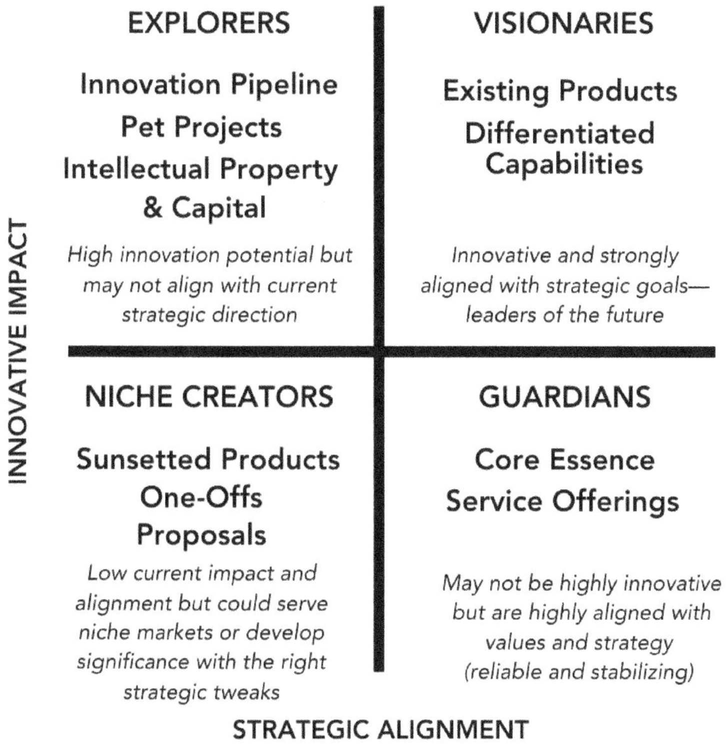

INNOVATIVE IMPACT

EXPLORERS	VISIONARIES
Innovation Pipeline **Pet Projects** **Intellectual Property & Capital** *High innovation potential but may not align with current strategic direction*	**Existing Products** **Differentiated Capabilities** *Innovative and strongly aligned with strategic goals—leaders of the future*
NICHE CREATORS	**GUARDIANS**
Sunsetted Products **One-Offs** **Proposals** *Low current impact and alignment but could serve niche markets or develop significance with the right strategic tweaks*	**Core Essence** **Service Offerings** *May not be highly innovative but are highly aligned with values and strategy (reliable and stabilizing)*

STRATEGIC ALIGNMENT

InnoMagination Asset Category Matrix

Collaboration Check

At the conclusion of each phase of the process, take time to effectively communicate to your core stakeholders and collaborators:

- Your objective(s) for this phase in the process and what you've accomplished (outline your methodology)
- What you have learned
- What challenges you have identified

- Any gaps in your sources of data or in resources needed
- Wins and recognition for key contributions
- Plans for the next phase with expected actions/activities
- Requests for feedback

Do this both by meeting and through documentation. The actual check-in session builds team cohesiveness and provides instant feedback.

Ensure you are presenting this data in a clear, concise, structured, and visually appealing manner and that it is easy and historically available for later reference. Your future self (at the business case stage of the process) will thank you for creating the foundation that supports the plan you present for final consensus and approval.

Tip: Remember, as you communicate throughout the ***InnoMagination*** process, everyone may not be gifted with futuristic vision. A wise leader at Accenture once counseled me. "You'll have to take some people along for your journey step-by-step so that they can see what you see and decide to take the journey with you to your Promised Land. Do not assume that everyone can make the mental leap multiple steps ahead." (Warning: Ignore this advice at your own peril.)

Phase 2: LANDSCAPE
Industry Insights: Fertile Grounds for Leveraging Existing Assets

> ***"The future belongs to those who see possibilities before they become obvious."***
>
> ***—John Sculley***

Section Objective: *Equip you to analyze and interpret macro and market dynamics using strategic tools so you can align existing assets with emerging external opportunities and drive* ***InnoMagination*** *grounded in real-world relevance.*

To innovate strategically, you must SEE the landscape clearly. The market doesn't exist in isolation...everything is connected.

In today's volatile and uncertain business environment, innovation isn't optional, it's essential. But true ***InnoMagination*** isn't about creating something brand new. You can leverage what you already have and reshape it to meet emerging needs, aligning it with the realities of your external environment.

The world around you—economic shifts, political dynamics, regulatory changes, social trends, technological advances—is the landscape upon which your organization grows. It impacts your strategy, influences your decisions, and inspires your ***InnoMagination***.

Let's SEE how the landscape shapes opportunity, SPARKS insights to leverage your existing assets, so that you can DO the strategic work to thrive.

Understanding Impact, Influence, and Inspiration

Before we dive deeper, let's clarify three essential concepts:

- **Impacts:** Direct, measurable effects on your business.
- **Influences:** Subtle shifts that gradually shape behaviors and decisions.
- **Inspiration:** The SPARK that drives you to innovate, create, and *InnoMaginate* possibilities.

For example, a new government regulation (tariffs, for example) directly impacts you by increasing costs. But shifting customer attitudes toward efficiency, cost-cutting, and sustainability might influence your company's culture and long-term decisions. These forces can become powerful inspirations and push you toward creative, strategic ***InnoMagination*** to turn challenges into opportunities.

Recognizing these distinctions helps you craft smarter strategies aligned with your landscape.

Exploring the Landscape: Fertile Grounds for *InnoMagination*

Economic Climate: The Resource Reality Check

In tight economic times, resources become scarce, budgets tighten, and investments shift toward refining and repositioning existing products. Are you fully leveraging your current assets to deliver more value at lower cost? Economic fluctuations aren't just obstacles. They're invitations (and opportunities) to innovate around efficiency, value delivery, and customer alignment.

In prosperous times, the landscape shifts again. Are you ready to seize opportunities when your customers are more open to risk and investment? SEE clearly, adjust quickly, and invest wisely.

Customer Behavior: Shifting Priorities, New Opportunities

Economic realities shape customer behavior. In downturns, customers prioritize essentials and cost-effectiveness. Your ***InnoMagination*** strategy should reflect that reality and deliver core value and smart pricing. When times are good, customers may seek ***InnoMagination*** that excites and differentiates.

Stay attuned to their shifting needs. Align your ***InnoMagination*** strategies with real customer priorities, and you'll SPARK deeper loyalty and sustainable success.

Political Climate: Navigating Change with Agility

Political uncertainty or regulatory shifts can quickly reshape your business landscape. Tariffs, trade policies, government budget impasses, data regulations...these changes can suddenly impact your product strategy and supply chain.

You can't control political shifts, but you can remain agile. Monitor developments closely, adapt quickly, and *InnoMaginate* your existing assets to navigate these challenges successfully.

International Relations: Turning Challenges into Competitive Advantages

Global relationships directly impact supply chains and market entry strategies. A new tariff or a geopolitical conflict could disrupt your plans overnight. But instead of seeing disruption as disaster, view it as an opportunity to innovate. This is the time to diversify your suppliers, explore new markets, or leverage technology to streamline operations.

Your ability to adapt quickly to changing international dynamics will set you apart. DO the strategic work to create flexible, resilient ***InnoMagination*** strategies.

Regulatory Impact: From Compliance Burden to *InnoMagination* Catalyst

Regulations like GDPR, CCPA, HIPAA, FedRAMP, or stricter environmental standards can seem daunting, adding compliance costs and complexity. But these challenges also SPARK ***InnoMagination***. They force you to rethink operations, data management, sustainability, and more.

Instead of treating compliance as merely a cost, SEE it as inspiration for innovative solutions. Turn regulatory requirements into competitive differentiation. Show customers you're ahead of the curve and committed to doing business the right way.

Social Responsibility: *InnoMagination* with Purpose

Consumers and investors today care deeply about social and

environmental issues. They expect businesses not just to profit but to contribute meaningfully to society. Companies that embrace sustainability and social responsibility aren't just doing good, they're doing smart business.

Align your ***InnoMagination*** strategies with these broader movements. SEE sustainability not as a constraint but as a powerful inspiration for ***InnoMagination*** and competitive advantage while doing the right thing.

Technological Advancements: Staying Ahead of the Curve

Technology evolves at warp speed, reshaping industries overnight. To stay competitive, you must invest in continuously understanding emerging technologies like AI and aligning them with your ***InnoMagination*** agenda.

Create a culture of continuous learning. Encourage your teams to explore emerging trends. DO the strategic work to integrate technology thoughtfully into your ***InnoMagination*** efforts, ensuring you stay agile, adaptive, and ahead of competitors.

The *InnoMagination* Process: Systematically Navigating the Landscape Phase

To effectively leverage your existing assets within the complex Landscape phase, here are a few of the tools we use in the structured ***InnoMagination*** process. While not the exhaustive list of Marketing, Management Consulting, and Innovation tools we employ to do an extensive deep dive, this set will provide you with enough knowledge to strongly understand your market and competitive environment:

1. PESTLE Analysis

Identify external political, economic, social, technological, legal, and environmental factors impacting your business. The PESTLE analysis aims to cut through the noise and provide a clear idea of the external environmental influences you must consider.

Rank the external PESTLE forces based on their potential impact, influence, and inspiration for your ***InnoMagination*** efforts.

2. Industry Scan

Conduct a thorough analysis of market forecasts, emerging and declining technologies, product trends, and competitive threats.

3. SWOTT Analysis

Perform an internal and external analysis of your strengths, weaknesses, opportunities, threats, and trends. Benchmark against competitors to ensure strategic alignment.

4. Five Forces Analysis

Use Porter's Five Forces framework to clearly understand your market position relative to competitors and industry pressures. This strategic model is used to assess the competitive dynamics of an industry. It looks at five key forces that shape profitability and market pressure: the threat of new entrants, the bargaining power of suppliers, the bargaining power of buyers, the threat of substitute products or services, and the level of competition among existing players.

Do this Landscape analysis process quarterly. Stay proactive. Align your ***InnoMagination*** strategy with a clear, nuanced understanding of your external landscape.

Navigating external forces can seem overwhelming. But these interconnected forces—economic, political, regulatory, social, technological, and environmental—don't just challenge your business. They also inspire transformative possibilities.

Instead of feeling constrained, SEE the connections clearly. SPARK new ideas from these insights. DO the strategic work to leverage your existing assets effectively and align them with your unique landscape.

Stop! Did you have a Collaboration Check?

Did you communicate:

- Your objective(s) for this phase in the process and what you've accomplished (outline your methodology)
- What you have learned
- What challenges you have identified
- Any gaps in your sources of data or in resources needed
- Wins and recognition for key contributions
- Plans for the next phase with expected actions/activities
- Requests for feedback

Phase 2: LANDSCAPE
Data-Driven Dreaming: The Role of Analytics in InnoMagination

> ***"Without data, you're just another person with an opinion."***
>
> — ***W. Edwards Deming***

Section Objective: *Show you how to use accessible, cost-effective analytics to uncover customer insights, validate opportunities, and guide* ***InnoMagination****, turning data into a strategic asset that powers informed, confident decision-making throughout the InnoMagination process.*

InnoMagination without data is guesswork. In today's environment, guessing just isn't good enough. But even with tight budgets and limited resources, you can leverage data strategically to guide your ***InnoMagination***. You don't need huge investments or massive teams, you just need a clear understanding of how data can illuminate untapped opportunities hidden within your existing assets.

Let's explore how data can become your strategic multiplier, enabling informed decisions and sparking powerful ***InnoMagination*** based on real insights.

Know Your Customer—Inside and Out

InnoMagination starts with deep customer insight. Fortunately, capturing these insights doesn't have to be complex or costly:

- **Internal Surveys & Frontline Feedback:** Engage your Sales, Customer Success, and front-line teams regularly. They see firsthand what's working, what's failing, and what customers genuinely want.

- **Leverage Public Platforms:** Use external sources like G2, StackOverflow, Reddit, Quora, and social media channels to uncover authentic customer sentiment. The insights you gain here are invaluable.

- **Sentiment Analysis Tools:** Affordable sentiment analysis tools can quickly reveal patterns in customer satisfaction and frustration, guiding your ***InnoMagination*** priorities clearly.

By deeply understanding your customers, you ensure every ***InnoMagination*** effort aligns directly with real market needs.

Rich Data—Without Breaking the Bank

You don't need deep pockets to gather deep insights. Smart, affordable strategies can deliver surprisingly rich data:

- **Web Scraping & Social Listening**: Free tools like Google Analytics and native analytics on platforms like Facebook, Instagram, and LinkedIn as well as some CRMs enable quick, powerful insights into customer behaviors and preferences.

- **Rapid Customer Feedback**: Platforms like Rapidr or Beamer help you capture quick, actionable customer insights, ensuring ***InnoMagination*** efforts stay closely aligned with real user needs.

- **Predictive Analytics on a Budget:** Even simple predictive analytics tools can anticipate customer trends, helping you proactively adapt and stay ahead of the market.

Simplify Data Collection—Quick, Actionable Insights

When your team is stretched thin, simplicity matters:

- **Direct Feedback Channels:** Collect quick, qualitative insights through email surveys or direct social media engagement.

- **Observational Research:** Simply observe how customers interact with your products. Often, the most revealing insights come from watching genuine user behavior.

Simplified data collection keeps you agile, responsive, and focused on high-impact insights.

Collaborate for Success—Partnerships That Pay Off

You don't have to do all the research alone. Build partnerships that amplify your capabilities:

- **AI Tools:** This is the quickest, easiest, and probably cheapest way to start. ChatGPT, Claude, Perplexity, and Google Gemini can rapidly synthesize market trends, analyze competitor landscapes, generate survey questions, interpret datasets, and simulate customer personas, enabling you to conduct preliminary research and stress-test ideas in minutes, at virtually no cost.

- **Local Universities & Tech Schools:** Students often seek real-world projects. Partnering with educational institutions gives you fresh perspectives and low-cost research. Some higher education institutions (community colleges and universities) even offer internships as short as one week that may correspond to your research needs.

- **Online Communities:** Industry forums and professional networks offer valuable insights, tools, and collaboration opportunities. Check out virtual or local in-person MeetUps for your Industry or topic of interest.

- **Platforms:** Fiverr, Upwork, Freelancer, Toptal, and PeoplePerHour give you on-demand access to skilled researchers, analysts, and data specialists who can quickly gather competitive intelligence, run surveys, scrape and organize datasets, or conduct user interviews, making them powerful, cost-effective tools for validating innovative ideas.

Collaboration multiplies your capabilities without draining resources.

Focus on Key Metrics—Less Noise, More Signal

You don't need to analyze everything. Just what truly matters:

- **Identify Core KPIs:** Focus on metrics directly tied to your ***InnoMagination*** objectives. Zeroing in reduces complexity and enhances clarity.

- **Prioritize Simplicity:** Streamline data collection and analysis to focus on meaningful insights that clearly inform strategic decisions.

Build Your Team's Skills—Internal Capabilities Drive *InnoMagination*

Your team might not include dedicated data analysts, but the team you do have possesses the potential to quickly develop essential skills:

- **Affordable Online Courses:** Platforms like Coursera, edX, and Khan Academy offer low-cost training to rapidly build your team's analytical capabilities. (In combination with AI tools, teams who understand the basics can manage the tools to handle your analytics needs.)

- **Webinars & Industry Workshops:** Short sessions can upgrade your team's skills, empowering confident ***InnoMagination*** and strategic decision-making.

Analyze Data Effectively—Turning Numbers into Action

Collecting data is only the first step. Turning it into actionable insights is where you win:

- **Centralize & Clean Data:** Consolidate your data, removing duplicates and errors.

- **Descriptive & Cross-Tab Analysis:** Identify clear patterns and trends, understanding how key metrics vary across different segments.

- **Qualitative Thematic Analysis:** Categorize qualitative insights into patterns that numbers alone can't reveal.

TIP: I once ran a Total Addressable Market (TAM) study for a global software company where qualitative insights illuminated hidden future potential in a region the numbers alone missed. The company was able to allocate resources ahead of plan to pursue that market. That region became a major revenue driver, proving marrying qualitative and quantitative data together creates powerful ***InnoMagination*** insights. Don't ignore **qualitative data** that may be identifying the 'next big thing'.

From Data to Decisive Action

Data alone doesn't drive ***InnoMagination***. You must add in decisive action and execution. In-between is analysis and strategy.

When used strategically, data empowers clarity, confidence, and informed action. It helps you SEE clearly, SPARK fresh ideas, and DO the strategic work to turn data into market-ready solutions.

Remember, data isn't your compass. That role belongs exclusively to your *Core Essence*. Instead, data is your trusted map, highlighting opportunities, navigating challenges, and aligning your strategy with your true organizational identity.

With the right insights, you'll not just dream, you'll dream strategically, innovate wisely, and execute decisively.

The *InnoMagination* Data Analysis Process

To systematically leverage data throughout your ***InnoMagination*** journey, follow these clear steps:

1. Identify Your Core KPIs

Clearly define the key metrics that directly align with your ***InnoMagination*** goals. (We'll cover this in detail in Phase 5 of this chapter).

2. Simplify Data Collection

Use cost-effective tools and straightforward methods to collect data quickly and clearly.

3. Analyze and Interpret

Centralize and clean your data, conduct descriptive and cross-tab analyses, and perform qualitative thematic analysis.

4. Collaborate and Leverage Partners

Partner with external organizations like universities, tech schools, or AI, online communities, or platforms to amplify your analytical capabilities.

5. Integrate and Act

Integrate insights into your ***InnoMagination*** strategy. Take clear, confident action based on real data to ensure your ***InnoMagination*** opportunity aligns with market realities and customer needs.

Perform this process regularly (quarterly is ideal) to keep ***InnoMagination*** strategically sharp, responsive, and market-aligned.

Leverage Data to Drive Strategic Action

Every data point you collect is a step toward smarter, clearer ***InnoMagination*** decisions. Data-driven insights aren't just for big teams or large budgets. With creativity and resourcefulness, even small teams can harness the power of analytics to identify market gaps, innovate effectively, and drive lasting growth.

Stop! Did you have a Collaboration Check?

Did you communicate:

- Your objective(s) for this phase in the process and what you've accomplished (outline your methodology)
- What you have learned
- What challenges you have identified
- Any gaps in your sources of data or in resources needed
- Wins and recognition for key contributions
- Plans for the next phase with expected actions/activities
- Requests for feedback

Phase 3: MARKETPLACE
The Voice of the Customer: Feedback as Fuel for InnoMagination

> ***"Your most unhappy customers are your greatest source of learning."***
>
> — ***Bill Gates***

Section Objective: *Show how to turn customer feedback into a strategic engine for* ***InnoMagination*** *by building intentional, cross-functional listening systems that transform voice-of-the-customer insights into actionable opportunities.*

InnoMagination that doesn't listen is ***InnoMagination*** that doesn't work.

If you're a growth-driven leader, you already know the weight of decisions—where to place your bets, when to pivot, and how to create something that truly matters. What if I told you the answers aren't hidden in a crystal ball or locked inside a strategy retreat? They're already around you, waiting to be heard.

Customer feedback isn't a nice-to-have. It's your most under-utilized ***InnoMagination*** asset. And it's closer than you think.

SEE the Feedback Hiding in Plain Sight

Imagine driving cross-country without a GPS using only intuition and occasional road signs. That's what it's like to innovate without listening to your customers. You might reach a destination, but it likely won't be the one you intended.

Feedback is more than opinions. It's data with heart. It reveals unmet needs, unexplored angles, and emerging desires. It helps you SEE not just where your offer is today, but where it needs to go next.

Think of it this way...every customer conversation is a breadcrumb. When you follow the trail, you uncover patterns—insights that have the power to shape strategy, refine products, and deepen loyalty.

SPARK *InnoMagination* by Listening Differently

Feedback flows through every layer of your business. It's in your inbox, your CRM, your support queue. But gathering it isn't enough. You've got to listen with intention. Not just for what's being said, but for what's being signaled.

Let's break it down:

- **Sales Conversations** reveal objections, decision-making patterns, and shifting priorities.

- **Customer Support Tickets** highlight friction points and recurring frustrations.

- **Renewal Rates & Churn** tell you whether your value proposition is sticky or slipping.

- **Product Usage Data** shows what's actually being used, not just what the customer thought they'd use.

Your job is to connect the dots. Don't treat these signals as isolated metrics. Treat them as puzzle pieces that, when assembled, reveal where ***InnoMagination*** is needed most.

CASE STUDY: Amazon Prime® – Innovation Fueled by the Voice of the Customer

Sometimes, the future isn't built from scratch—it's repackaged from what's already working, just waiting to be seen through a new lens.

That's exactly what Amazon did with Prime.

Customers weren't asking for a subscription. They were asking for something simpler: faster, more affordable shipping. Amazon already had the infrastructure. What they didn't have—yet—was the packaging.

By listening closely to customer frustrations about shipping speed and delivery costs, Amazon uncovered an opportunity hiding in plain sight. They didn't need to build something new. They needed to reimagine what they already had.

Enter Amazon Prime—a category-defining membership model that bundled two things customers deeply cared about: speed and savings. What started as a logistics innovation quickly became a loyalty engine.

The brilliance wasn't just in the service itself—it was in the strategic repackaging of existing capabilities based on customer feedback. Prime turned operational efficiency into a premium product. It added value without adding complexity. And it sparked a behavioral shift—customers began buying more, more often, with greater brand loyalty.

But the innovation didn't stop there. Amazon continued listening. Over time, they layered in new benefits—streaming, exclusive deals, grocery delivery—expanding the membership's meaning and deepening its relevance in customers' lives–all benefits that add value and reduce the rate of churn.

The takeaway?
Listening to your customers doesn't just improve experience—it can spark a business model transformation. Amazon didn't just meet expectations. They reset them—for an entire industry. [48]

This is customer-centric innovation at its finest:

SEE the unspoken desires.
SPARK an idea using what you already have.
DO the work to deliver it in a way that adds exponential value.

DO the Work: Build Feedback Loops That Drive Strategy

To make the most of customer insight, you need more than a suggestion box. You need a system.

Here's how to build one:

1. Create Multi-Point Listening Channels

Collect feedback across the entire customer journey, from pre-sale to onboarding and usage through renewal. Every stage reveals something different. Learn why they are or why they are not buying, if they are having difficulties in the onboarding process, what features they are or are not using, use cases that may differ from the product's designed purpose, why they are or are not renewing, customer wishlist items, etc.

HOW MAJOR BRANDS USE VoC FOR INNOVATION:

Lego®: Innovation, Crowdsourced

Lego didn't just open the door to customer feedback—they gave customers a seat at the design table.

Through the Lego Ideas Platform®, fans from around the world submit their own set designs. If enough people vote, Lego reviews the idea for potential production. That's not just engagement—that's innovation at scale.

This feedback loop does more than collect ideas. It builds community. It fosters co-creation. And it gives Lego a direct line into what their most passionate users want next.

Lego shows us that when you empower customers to help shape the product, you don't just create better toys—you create lifelong fans. [49]

2. Centralize and Share

Use a shared dashboard or workspace where feedback is documented, categorized, and accessible across teams. A searchable, historical record is an ideal tool to break down silos and foster cross-functional collaboration.

HOW MAJOR BRANDS USE VoC FOR INNOVATION:
Zappos®: Customer Service as a Business Model

Zappos didn't just listen to customers—they built a culture around it.

From fast, free shipping to a 365-day return policy, Zappos turned every customer interaction into a moment of trust. But their real differentiator? The freedom their support team has to make things right, without scripts or rigid rules.

They mine insights from every call, tweet, and email—not just to fix problems, but to reimagine their service playbook. Feedback isn't a metric at Zappos—it's a movement.

By treating service as a conversation—not a transaction—Zappos turned loyalty into a lifestyle. [50]

Zappos was acquired by Amazon in 2009.

3. Measure What Matters

Track key indicators like Net Promoter Score (NPS), customer effort score, renewal rate, and feature adoption. But don't stop at numbers—pair them with qualitative insights to tell the full story.

HOW MAJOR BRANDS USE VoC FOR INNOVATION:

Netflix®: Turning Patterns into Personalization

For Netflix, every click tells a story. And every story sparks strategy.

By analyzing customer behavior—what we watch, pause, skip, or binge—Netflix continuously refines its recommendation engine. But it doesn't stop there. These insights also shape what the company creates. Customer feedback fuels content decisions, guiding Netflix toward greenlighting shows that align with emerging viewer preferences.

The result? More relevance, more retention, and a content engine that feels deeply personal—even at scale.

Netflix proves that feedback isn't just about improving what exists—it's about inspiring what's next. [51]

4. Create a Customer Advisory Board (CAB)

Bring together a curated group of customers who represent diversity in size, industry, and use case. Meet quarterly. Share your roadmap. Ask bold questions. Listen deeply.

A well-run CAB doesn't just validate your direction. It challenges it. And that's exactly what you want. Because when your customers help shape the future, they're far more likely to stay part of it.

HOW MAJOR BRANDS USE VoC FOR INNOVATION:

Apple®: Designing with the End User in the Room

Apple's secret isn't just sleek design—it's strategic listening.

From the earliest days of the iPod to today's iPhone features like Face ID and Siri, Apple has made a habit of transforming user frustrations into innovation gold. Customers wanted a faster way to unlock their phones, a smarter way to multitask, a more intuitive way to connect—and Apple delivered, not by guessing, but by listening.

Behind the scenes, Apple collects feedback through user experience research, direct support conversations, and behavioral analytics. But what sets them apart? They don't just hear what users say—they anticipate what they mean. That's how they build features people didn't know they needed... until they couldn't live without them.

Apple doesn't just design for customers. They design with them—by putting feedback at the center of the product experience. [52]

This Is Intentional Strategy

Let's drop the myth that customer feedback slows down ***InnoMagination***. Actually, the opposite is true. Listening speeds up clarity. It helps you avoid building things no one wants. It de-risks your roadmap. It transforms your customers into co-creators.

If ***InnoMagination*** is your rocket, feedback is your fuel.

Don't just collect it. Act on it. Let it shape your next iteration, your next big bet, your next bold move.

HOW MAJOR BRANDS USE VoC FOR INNOVATION:

Samsung®: Listening That Shapes the Specs

Samsung doesn't just respond to trends—they listen for them.

Take the Galaxy S9. Customer feedback revealed a consistent, annoying challenge: mobile photography in low light. In response, Samsung developed a dual-aperture camera that automatically adjusted to lighting conditions—a feature directly inspired by user behavior and preferences.

Their approach blends deep market research, UX testing, and fast feedback cycles to ensure new products aren't just technically advanced—but emotionally resonant.

Samsung proves that when you build with the user's voice in mind, you don't just add features—you add value. [53]

The marketplace isn't silent. It's speaking...through every click, complaint, compliment, and cancellation.

Your competitive edge isn't just about who has the best ideas. It's about who's listening best...and who's willing to act on what they hear.

Feedback is more than opinion, it's direction. It's strategy. It's the fastest way to align your ***InnoMagination*** with what matters most.

So lean in. Listen closer.

The voice of your customer just might be the voice of your next breakthrough.

Stop! Did you have a Collaboration Check?

Did you communicate:

- Your objective(s) for this phase in the process and what you've accomplished (outline your methodology)
- What you have learned
- What challenges you have identified
- Any gaps in your sources of data or in resources needed
- Wins and recognition for key contributions
- Plans for the next phase with expected actions/activities
- Requests for feedback

Phase 3: MARKETPLACE
Scenarios, Market Gaps & Unmet Needs! Oh My!

> ***"Understanding human needs is half the job of meeting them."***
>
> ***— Adlai E. Stevenson***

Section Objective: *Equip leaders with tools to uncover strategic opportunities and enable faster, lower-risk* ***InnoMagination*** *by aligning existing assets with evolving market realities.*

The future isn't something you predict, it's something you prepare for, by clearly seeing scenarios, spotting unmet needs, and uncovering hidden market gaps.

At this stage in our ***InnoMagination*** journey, you're beginning to see precisely how your strengths, assets, and products can align strategically with emerging opportunities. But don't get started on that just yet. Strategic ***InnoMagination*** requires discipline—pausing intentionally to explore possibilities, challenge assumptions, and clarify where hidden opportunities lie.

Let's talk about three powerful routes for refining your ***InnoMagination*** focus: *Scenario Analysis, Market Gaps, and Unmet Customer Needs.*

Scenario Analysis: Preparing Strategically for Multiple Futures

Your ***InnoMagination*** plans shouldn't be built by guessing about the future. Designing your plans is rooted in preparing for multiple plausible futures. Scenario analysis is your tool for navigating uncertainty. By systematically exploring different potential futures, you uncover hidden opportunities and proactively mitigate risks.

Here's how to perform a scenario analysis:

1. Identify Your Key Drivers of Change

Revisit your earlier Landscape analysis. Clearly define factors shaping your market including technology shifts, regulatory changes, evolving customer behaviors, competitive movements, or geopolitical events. Each could dramatically reshape your ***InnoMagination*** landscape.

2. Develop Multiple Strategic Scenarios

Don't just imagine one future. Explore several:

- **Base-case scenario (*status quo*):** What happens if current trends continue?
- **Best-case scenario:** What if things go exceptionally well?
- **Worst-case scenario:** What if the market takes an unexpected downturn?
- **Most-likely scenario:** What's realistically probable, given current data? (This might be a combination of any of the above or something quite different.)

Craft detailed narratives around each scenario. How would customers respond? How would competitors shift? What new gaps or unmet needs emerge?

3. Evaluate Implications Clearly
Analyze scenarios to tease out implications. Ask clearly:

- What gaps become visible?
- What unmet needs emerge?
- Where could your existing capabilities shine brightest?

This helps you pinpoint exactly where your ***InnoMagination*** can yield maximum impact.

4. Prioritize Aligned Opportunities
Not every scenario deserves equal attention. Prioritize scenarios that align best with your *Core Essence*, focusing on your existing strengths, capabilities, and strategic direction. Leverage scenarios that position you to deliver unique value and competitive advantage.

Market Gaps: Hidden Opportunities in Plain Sight

Market gaps are underserved spaces where customer needs remain unmet or inadequately addressed. These are places ripe for ***InnoMagination***. Mature companies facing slow growth often overlook these hidden opportunities. Yet, the greatest potential often exists precisely in these overlooked spaces.

Here's how to identify those gaps clearly:

1. Dig into Market Research
Mine your data—market reports, sales trends, analytics, and surveys—to uncover underserved segments or emerging preferences. Don't limit yourself to your immediate industry; adjacent markets can uncover surprising new potential.

2. Listen Deeply to Customers

Customers know their own pain points intimately. Listen beyond surface-level feedback. Utilize focus groups, social listening, and direct interactions to help reveal deeper frustrations and unmet desires. This is your direct line to meaningful ***InnoMagination***.

3. Study Competitors Strategically

Look closely at competitors, not just to copy, but to identify blind spots. What features or services are they neglecting? Where do their customers still feel friction? Competitors' shortcomings often signal prime ***InnoMagination*** opportunities.

4. Explore Adjacent Markets

Don't stay trapped within existing boundaries. Look at adjacent markets or related industries. Often, your existing capabilities can solve problems in entirely new customer segments, opening fresh opportunities without significant investment.

CASE STUDY: How We Turned a Market Gap into Market Leadership at Verizon Wireless®

When I took on leading the National Government Marketing team at Verizon Wireless, we already had a powerful reputation for reliability—but we had historically overlooked one critical market: Public Safety. Despite our core strength of superior network reliability, a major competitor dominated this space, leaving us stuck outside, looking in.

Looking back at the prior few years, I realized that two major crises—9/11 and Hurricane Katrina—exposed a clear, urgent market gap. First responders were frustrated with unreliable emergency communications and people were dying because of inadequate communications between first responder teams. The need was undeniable, and existing solutions weren't meeting expectations.

I recognized an opening: our competitor's push-to-talk (PTT) technology was about to lose its patent protection. Suddenly, we had an opportunity perfectly aligned with Verizon's stated value of "running to a crisis, not away from it", our brand promise of the most reliable network, the mission of creating networks that move the world forward, an organizational personality of trusted, caring support, and strategic direction set by the executive teams.

We assembled a cross-functional team to rapidly leverage those strengths. Instead of inventing something entirely new, we strategically reimagined, repositioned, and repackaged the soon-to-be off-patent technology, creating a specialized solution tailored specifically for first responders. We focused sharply on the market gap—delivering exactly what our customers urgently needed.

The result? Verizon Wireless rapidly became the new leader in Public Safety wireless communications.

This experience created the core principle at the heart of the ***InnoMagination*** framework: innovation doesn't always mean invention. Often, your greatest opportunities lie in clearly seeing market gaps and strategically leveraging what you already have to fill them.

Unmet Needs: Your Customer's Unspoken Desires

Unmet needs aren't always obvious, yet they represent powerful ***InnoMagination*** possibilities. These needs often exist beneath the surface, waiting for someone insightful enough to notice.

Here's how to uncover them effectively:

1. Develop Rich User Personas

Create detailed profiles beyond simple demographics. Capture Jobs-To-Be-Done, motivations, habits, frustrations, and aspirations. Include adjacent or overlooked customer segments. Your future growth might lie there.

2. Map the Customer Journey Clearly

Walk through your customer's entire experience with fresh eyes. Where are they experiencing friction or frustration? Which steps are causing hesitation or dissatisfaction? Identifying these moments can illuminate valuable unmet needs.

3. Conduct Pain Point Analysis
Pay close attention to recurring complaints, frustrations, and requests. The problems your customers repeatedly highlight signal areas where meaningful ***InnoMagination*** can generate immediate value and loyalty.

Leverage Existing Assets for Faster *InnoMagination*
InnoMagination doesn't always mean building something new from scratch. Your quickest route to market often is repurposing or repositioning what you already have.

To recap so far, here's how to innovate swiftly using your existing resources:

1. Audit Your Current Assets
Review the comprehensive inventory you've created in Chapter 11. Which capabilities or products are under-utilized ? Which could quickly serve unmet needs if repositioned?

2. *InnoMagine* & Reposition Creatively
Brainstorm creatively. Could you bundle products differently, target new audiences, or adapt features slightly for fresh use cases? Simple shifts can create significant value.

3. Test & Validate Rapidly
Prototype rapidly and test early. Gather feedback from real customers quickly to refine your offering before a full-scale launch. The trusted customers in your CAB are excellent resources for feedback on your proposed ideas and prototypes.

4. Iterate Based on Real-World Insights

Use marketing analytics, customer feedback, and early user behavior to sharpen your market positioning. Employ Agile[1] iteration to ensure continuous alignment with evolving customer expectations.

CASE STUDY: What Happens When You Ignore Market Gaps—Lessons from BlackBerry®

BlackBerry used to dominate the wireless device market. They were everywhere—trusted by business professionals worldwide for secure messaging, reliable service, and an iconic physical keyboard. BlackBerry was unstoppable—or so it seemed.

But they missed something crucial. As consumer preferences rapidly shifted toward touchscreen smartphones and robust app ecosystems, BlackBerry clung firmly to their traditional keyboard-centric devices. The market gap was clear: customers increasingly wanted intuitive touchscreen devices and the vibrant ecosystems of apps that could enhance productivity and lifestyle. Over time, they'd lost their 'cool' factor.

Yet BlackBerry resisted adapting. Rather than clearly seeing and strategically responding to these unmet needs, they doubled down on what had always worked before.

---

1. Note: The Agile process is an iterative, cyclical software development approach that involves repeated cycles of planning, development, testing, and feedback, enabling quick, easy, continuous improvement.

The consequences were swift—and severe. Competitors like Apple and Android® eagerly filled the gaps BlackBerry ignored. They innovated quickly, offering touchscreen devices and thriving app marketplaces that customers embraced enthusiastically. Almost overnight, BlackBerry's market leadership evaporated. Revenues plummeted. Their brand lost relevance.

Their story reinforces a powerful strategic lesson: ignoring clear market gaps isn't just a missed opportunity—it's a direct pathway to obsolescence. To thrive, innovation must always start by clearly seeing and courageously addressing unmet market needs, even when it is an inconvenient truth. [54]

Scenario analysis, market gap identification, and uncovering unmet needs aren't separate exercises. They're interconnected tools for strategic clarity. Together, they guide you toward smarter, more impactful ***InnoMagination*** decisions—leveraging existing strengths and enabling faster, lower-risk growth.

The future doesn't belong to companies that guess best—it belongs to those prepared to pivot, adapt, and innovate strategically. This is how you uncover hidden opportunities clearly—and how you confidently make your next move.

Stop! Did you have a Collaboration Check?

Did you communicate:

- Your objective(s) for this phase in the process and what you've accomplished (outline your methodology)

- What you have learned
- What challenges you have identified
- Any gaps in your sources of data or in resources needed
- Wins and recognition for key contributions
- Plans for the next phase with expected actions/activities
- Requests for feedback

Phase 4: PURSUIT
Risk Less, Achieve More: Strategically Evaluating Your Options

> ***"Strategy is about making choices, trade-offs; it's about deliberately choosing to be different."***
>
> ***— Michael Porter***

Section Objective: *Provide a clear, data-informed framework for evaluating* ***InnoMagination*** *opportunities to reduce risk, accelerate* *speed-to-market, and align cross-functional teams through leveraging existing assets.*

Innovation can be thrilling, but honestly, it can also feel a little risky. What if the market rejects your idea? What if the costs spiral out of control? How do you convince your teams to embrace the uncertainty? These questions can paralyze even the most visionary leaders.

But the good news is ***InnoMagination*** doesn't have to mean starting your innovation exercise from scratch or betting the farm. By strategically leveraging your existing assets, you can reduce risk, accelerate speed-to-market, and boost internal alignment, transforming ***InnoMagination*** from a gamble into a calculated pursuit.

Let me walk you through how to approach it.

Proven Value Reduces Market Risk

As Jim Rohn famously stated, "Success leaves clues." Your existing products and services aren't just revenue streams—they're proof points. You've already built trust, credibility, and market acceptance. When you innovate by building upon your proven successes, you turn ***InnoMagination*** into a logical, customer-centric evolution, rather than a risky leap into the unknown.

Effective marketing isn't shouting into the void; it's clearly connecting ***InnoMagination*** to reliability, familiarity, and trust. When customers see ***InnoMagination*** as a logical evolution—not a radical leap—they feel safe to embrace it.

In short, customers trust what's familiar. Position your ***InnoMagination*** clearly as an extension of your existing success, and you'll dramatically reduce the risk of rejection.

De-Risk Development by Leveraging Existing Assets

InnoMagination doesn't have to mean massive risk. Often, your smartest move is strategic repositioning—extending existing offerings into new areas customers already trust. This balance reduces risk perception, eases internal fears, and improves adoption rates.

Starting from scratch might feel "innovative", but it's often unnecessarily risky. The smartest ***InnoMagination*** opportunities start by reimagining what's already working. Consider Spanx. They didn't invent shapewear (the earliest record dates shapewear-like garments back to the Minoans around 1600 BCE); they saw an unmet need and improved an existing concept. By leveraging existing market-available products, Spanx reduced R&D costs, accelerated their timeline, and minimized resource drain.

Today, Spanx's annual revenue is approximately $150-$160 million.[55]

Think clearly about your current portfolio. Often, your greatest ***InnoMagination*** potential lives in adapting, repositioning, or extending existing offerings, minimizing risk while maximizing impact.

Accelerate Speed-to-Market

InnoMagination often comes down to timing. Too early, and the market isn't ready; too late, and you've missed your moment. Leveraging existing products accelerates your speed-to-market. You're not starting from zero; you're enhancing, repositioning, or adapting what's already proven.

Customers already have relationships with your current products. Positioning your ***InnoMagination*** clearly within a familiar context helps seamlessly transition customers from what they already love to what's next.

Foster Cultural and Organizational Alignment

InnoMagination requires internal buy-in; it doesn't happen in isolation. Your teams must feel confident to experiment, explore, and embrace uncertainty. Leveraging your existing strengths gives your employees confidence, providing a stable foundation that encourages creative risk-taking.

Your teams must also be empowered to take risks and experiment. (We'll talk more about this a little later).

Clear alignment around proven assets creates internal momentum. When employees trust the foundation beneath their feet, they feel empowered to innovate boldly. This creates a ripple effect of confidence and creativity throughout your organization.

Evaluating *InnoMagination* Opportunities: The Opportunity Assessment Wheel

How do you objectively evaluate ***InnoMagination*** opportunities? The ***InnoMagination*** framework guides you clearly through the six key indicators of the *Opportunity Assessment Wheel* to assess feasibility, viability, and strategic alignment:

1. Consolidated Financial Assessment

Evaluate your resources clearly:

- **Costs and Effort:** What's the investment required financially and operationally? Is it feasible given your resources?
- **Timeline Feasibility:** Can you realistically hit market windows and the time to ROI required? If not, reconsider before investing.
- **ROI Projection:** Estimate potential revenue clearly. Does the expected return justify the investment?

2. Market Fit

Evaluate market demand clearly. Does your *InnoMagined* offering align with emerging trends and customer needs? Does it offer clear competitive differentiation?

3. Risk Assessment

Clearly analyze internal and external risks. Identify potential roadblocks, competitive responses, or market shifts. Mitigate or eliminate potential risks proactively to maximize your chances of success.

4. Strategic Alignment with Core Strengths

Does the opportunity align clearly with your proven strengths and capabilities? ***InnoMagination*** that leverages your existing expertise ensures faster success and greater internal alignment.

5. Speed-to-Market Execution

Can you quickly develop, test, and launch without sacrificing quality? Clear, rapid execution ensures market timing aligns strategically with customer readiness.

6. Change Readiness

Assess your organization's readiness clearly. Are teams aligned and prepared? Is your organization culturally positioned to rapidly adapt and innovate?

Applying Weighted Scoring to Prioritize Clearly

After evaluating these six indicators, assign each indicator a weighted score based on strategic importance to your organization (for example, on a scale of 1–10). Multiply each indicator score by an assigned weight you've determined. This creates a clear, objective comparative framework for assessing each potential opportunity.

For instance, if *Market Fit* scores 8 (high), and its weight is 25% out of a total of 100%, its weighted contribution is 2.0 (8 x 0.25). Summing these weighted scores provides an objective, comprehensive evaluation of your ***InnoMagination*** opportunities.

Use these weighted scores to create an ***Opportunity Assessment Wheel***, visualizing comparative strengths and weaknesses between opportunities you are considering to clearly prioritize options to pursue.

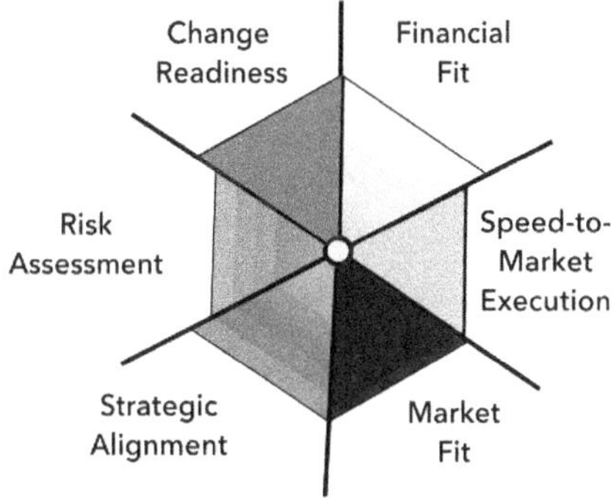

Opportunity Assessment Wheel

Strategic Clarity, Confident *InnoMagination*

InnoMagination doesn't operate via reckless risk or guesswork. With the ***InnoMagination*** framework, you clearly leverage existing strengths, objectively assess opportunities, and strategically pursue ***InnoMagination***, reducing risk and maximizing reward.

And when you innovate strategically—grounded in clear analysis and proven assets—you confidently position your organization for faster growth, deeper market trust, and stronger internal alignment.

Remember, your existing strengths aren't limitations; they're strategic assets. Leverage them wisely, and ***InnoMagination*** becomes your powerful competitive advantage.

Stop! Did you have a Collaboration Check?

Did you communicate:

- Your objective(s) for this phase in the process and what you've accomplished (outline your methodology)
- What you have learned
- What challenges you have identified
- Any gaps in your sources of data or in resources needed
- Wins and recognition for key contributions
- Plans for the next phase with expected actions/activities
- Requests for feedback

Phase 5: OFFER
Collaboration in Action: Cross-Functional Teams & Change Management

> ***"Coming together is a beginning, staying together is progress, and working together is success."***
>
> — ***Henry Ford***

Section Objective: *Establish cross-functional collaboration and intentional change management as non-negotiable elements of **InnoMagination**, demonstrating how Marketing can lead alignment, drive execution, and embed a culture of co-creation across the organization through the InnoMagination framework.*

InnoMagination isn't a department. It's how your organization gets things done together.

Collaboration is the very engine of ***InnoMagination***. Without it, you'll find it very difficult to make much progress in your ***InnoMagination*** journey.

Let me share my experience and how I learned this very valuable lesson.

When I was at Verizon Wireless, the idea that eventually became the ***InnoMagination™*** framework didn't come from a whiteboard session or a strategy retreat. It came from a rare moment of convergence—when unmet customer need, untapped internal capability, and market timing all aligned in a way few people were paying attention to.

We didn't need to invent something from scratch.

We needed to repackage **what we already had**, reposition it strategically, and move fast—before anyone else saw the gap.

But this wasn't a "go rogue and hope" kind of story.

We were in a highly regulated, risk-averse industry, working within the context of Federal government buyers, policy constraints, and a legacy corporate culture where change didn't exactly move at the speed of ambition.

The idea was bold. And bold ideas don't land unless they're sold.

So, I started selling.

First, to my boss. He saw the potential and gave me the air cover to go further. Together, we brought it (with the research data and business case) to his peers, then up the chain to his boss, the head of the Government business. Once we had C-level buy-in, I turned sideways—to Product, Sales, Legal, Finance, Operations, and Government Relations.

Some people got it right away. Some were reluctant. Some were flat-out skeptical.

But I kept going. Kept listening. Kept adjusting. Kept bringing people in.

Eventually, I was able to work with HQ and cross-functional national teams to turn the spark into a shared vision. And slowly, something powerful started to happen:

The idea became **ours**, not mine.

People refined it. Challenged it. Strengthened it.
It gained advocates. It gained traction. And eventually, it gained a life of its own.

There's a quote by 5th-century BCE sage, Lao Tzu, in the *Tao Te Ching* that describes the highest form of leadership:

"A leader is best when people barely know he exists.
When his work is done, his aim is fulfilled, they will say:
we did it ourselves."

That's when I knew the vision had truly succeeded.

Because when people co-create something, they don't just execute it.

They champion it. They protect it. They build on it like it's their own—because of course, now, it **IS**.

Not surface-level alignment. Deep, emotional ownership.

Across functions. Across boundaries. Across the org chart.

That's why collaboration isn't just a step in the process. It's the engine itself.

It's what transforms an idea into a movement.

It's what turns Marketing from a messenger into a maker.

And it's exactly what ***InnoMagination*** is designed to empower.

InnoMagination really has outgrown the old model of isolated R&D labs and "skunkworks" teams. Today's pace of change demands something deeper, something more visceral: true cross-functional collaboration. The reality is, most companies aren't built for this. They're designed for efficiency, predictability, and protecting what's already successful. (Remember the *Legacy Lock Contradiction*?) Those strengths, ironically, often become barriers to meaningful innovation.

That's why I created the ***InnoMagination*** framework. It is a practical way to operationalize collaboration for innovation across your entire organization. It provides structure, clarity, and direction, enabling teams to innovate together without confusion or chaos.

Why Marketing Should Lead *InnoMagination* (and It's Not Just Because I've Been a Marketing Leader)

Traditionally, Marketing teams are seen as the final step in getting a product launched: they're handed the finished product to package and sell, like the last stop on a factory conveyor belt. But here's the truth I learned firsthand at Verizon Wireless: Marketing *uniquely* sits at the intersection of customer insight, internal capabilities, and strategic storytelling. Marketing sees what's missing in the market first. It clearly understands organizational assets that might be overlooked. And it knows how to frame opportunities in ways that resonate both internally and externally.

In the ***InnoMagination*** world, Marketing steps into a new, proactive role. Not to take credit, but to clearly orchestrate collaboration. Marketing becomes the convener, the translator, and the strategic driver connecting dots between customer needs, business strategy, and execution.

How *InnoMagination* Makes Cross-Functional Work Real

Frankly, I'll admit cross-functional collaboration often sounds great but rarely works smoothly. Meetings multiply, accountability blurs, and momentum slows. I've seen it happen again and again.

InnoMagination addresses this directly by clearly structuring collaboration across defined phases, each designed to leverage different teams' expertise while keeping Marketing at the center to maintain clarity and momentum:

- **IDENTITY Phase**: Strategy*, RevOps, Product, Customer Experience (CX) & Insights, and Customer Success/Support teams surface core internal strengths. Marketing clearly leads the discovery and distills these insights into the foundation for innovation.

- **LANDSCAPE Phase:** Strategy*, Product, Sales, RevOps, Pricing, Customer Experience & Insights, and Customer Success/Support teams contribute external market realities. But Marketing does the deep dive and synthesizes this information clearly into actionable opportunities.

- **MARKETPLACE Phase:** Strategy*, Product, Sales, RevOps, Pricing, Customer Experience & Insights, and certain Ops teams identify unmet customer needs. Marketing translates these insights into clear innovation priorities.

- **PURSUIT Phase:** Strategy*, Finance, Operations, RevOps, Pricing, Product, PMO, QA, and certain Ops teams evaluate ideas for feasibility and risk. Marketing ensures clarity around market fit remains central, keeping ideas grounded in real customer value, not internal bias.

- **OFFER Phase & Launch:** Marketing orchestrates final positioning, messaging, and Go-To-Market execution across Product, Sales, Customer Experience & Insights, PMO, QA, Finance, Pricing, and Customer Success/Support teams and stakeholders, converting cross-functional input into tangible, customer-facing solutions.

*NOTE: In organizations without a Strategy function, this role can be assumed by Product Marketing or Market Insights personnel. Executive leadership is involved in each phase.

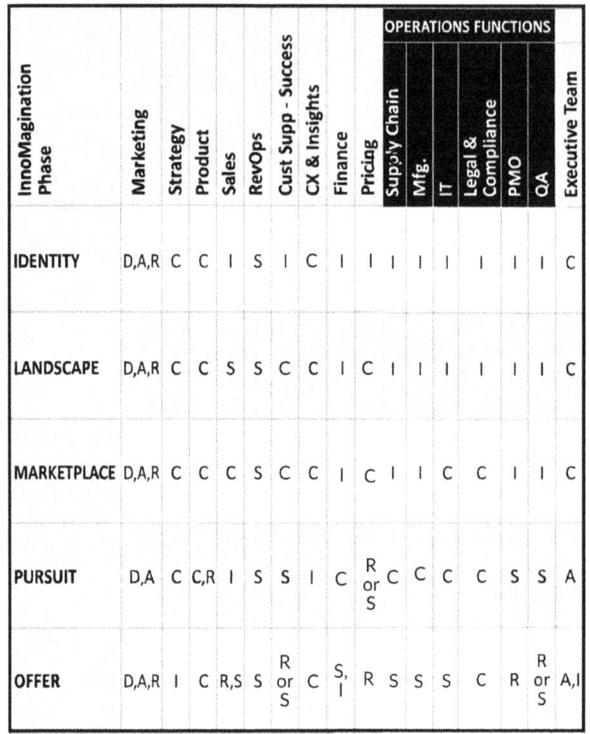

InnoMagination Phase	Marketing	Strategy	Product	Sales	RevOps	Cust Supp - Success	CX & Insights	Finance	Pricing	OPERATIONS FUNCTIONS						Executive Team
										Supply Chain	Mfg.	IT	Legal & Compliance	PMO	QA	
IDENTITY	D,A,R	C	C	I	S	I	C	I	I	I	I	I	I	I	I	C
LANDSCAPE	D,A,R	C	C	S	S	C	C	I	C	I	I	I	I	I	I	C
MARKETPLACE	D,A,R	C	C	C	S	C	C	I	C	I	I	C	C	I	I	C
PURSUIT	D,A	C	C,R	I	S	S	I	C	R or S	C	C	C	C	S	S	A
OFFER	D,A,R	I	C	R,S	S	R or S	C	S, I	R	S	S	S	C	R	R or S	A,I

Comprehensive DRASCI Matrix of InnoMagination

DRASCI definitions:

D (Driver): Delegates and steers execution

R (Responsible): Does the work

A (Accountable): Owns success/failure; has final approval

S (Support): Provides assistance, resources, or hands-on help

C (Consulted): Provides opinion, experience, and input before decisions or actions

I (Informed): Kept updated on progress and outcomes

NOTES:

- Marketing remains the central hub (Driver, Accountable, and Responsible), orchestrating each phase clearly.

- Operations-related groups (Supply Chain, Manufacturing, IT, Legal/Compliance, PMO, Customer Service, QA) have clearly defined roles, typically "Support" (S), "Consulted" (C) when their expertise directly impacts feasibility, risk, or execution, and "Informed" (I) when their involvement is about awareness and alignment.

The Change Management Imperative: Innovation Means Change
Here's something I've learned over and over in my career: Innovation always means change, and change can be uncomfortable, which ultimately means *innovation* can be uncomfortable. It disrupts routines, threatens identities, and creates uncertainty. Yet, somehow, many organizations consistently underestimate the emotional cost of innovation.

In addition to being a new way to look at innovation, ***InnoMagination*** is also a practical guide for managing the human side of change.

Here's how to clearly and intentionally build change management into the process to make it easier and less uncomfortable for all. Begin with the following steps:

1. Perform a Change Readiness Assessment
Assess each stakeholder's readiness:

- **Change Ready:** Energized by possibility
- **Change Resistant:** Skeptical and protective of the *status quo*
- **Change Fatigued:** Overloaded from too much change too quickly

Determine where your organization (on the team and individual stakeholder levels) sits on the change spectrum. This clarity will help you engage stakeholders and teams across the business thoughtfully and proactively.

2. Create a Stakeholder Map

Stakeholder mapping is a strategy-driven approach to identifying everyone affected by a change initiative. It helps you pinpoint who holds influence, who needs to be engaged, and how to tailor communication to build alignment and momentum across all stakeholder groups.

a. Start by identifying everyone impacted, not just obvious players like Sales or Product, but also overlooked functions like Legal, Compliance, and Operations. (See the DRASCI Matrix above.)

b. Define roles and assign to each key stakeholder and stakeholder group:

- Decision-maker, Influencer, Implementer, End User

c. Assess the level of influence and impact of each key stakeholder or stakeholder group

- **High Influence:** Individuals or groups with the authority to shape outcomes, such as key decision-makers, executive sponsors, or major influencers.

- **Moderate Influence:** Stakeholders who support execution or influence specific components of the initiative but don't control the overall direction.

- **Low Influence:** Those who are indirectly impacted and have limited control, yet whose awareness or support can still contribute to success.

d. Determine the best engagement strategy for each stakeholder group

- **Close Management:** Involve them as key champions of the initiative, securing their full support and ensuring they're aligned with the project's objectives.
- **Keep Satisfied:** Sustain their support and positive perception by keeping them engaged, ensuring their influence is used strategically to advance the initiative.
- **Keep Informed:** Keep them informed and inspired, equipping them with just enough knowledge to stay engaged, without requiring active involvement.
- **Monitor:** Ensure they have baseline awareness of the initiative and stay ready to engage more deeply if their interest or influence increases.

This process will enable you to know how to prioritize your efforts and adapt your communication strategies based on each stakeholder's level of interest and influence. This isn't political at all; it's strategic precision. It ensures definite alignment, early buy-in, and fewer surprises downstream.

3. Prepare, Manage, and Sustain the Change

Structure your approach to managing change:

- **Prepare:** Explicitly define success, anticipate resistance, communicate openly.
- **Manage:** Equip your teams with skills and context. Communicate transparently and consistently about what's

changing, why it matters, and what's in it for them.

- **Sustain:** Reinforce new behaviors, celebrate quick wins, and embed the changes into organizational culture, beyond slide decks and memos.

Organizational change succeeds one person at a time.

If individuals don't adapt how they work day-to-day, even the most ambitious transformation will fall short.

Poorly managed change comes at a high cost—lower morale, missed deadlines, blown budgets, rework, and even project failure.

On the flip side, strong change management dramatically improves outcomes and are more likely to achieve their objectives than those that struggle with it.

It is worth the time and effort to manage change carefully. It will take you longer to clean up the damage of rushing through it than it will to do it right the first time.

From Collaboration to Culture Shift

Collaboration shouldn't be an event. Collaboration MUST become your organization's natural way of working. Over time, collaboration builds trust, alignment, and clarity. It creates a healthier, more resilient organization that is fully equipped to tackle future changes with confidence.

When teams truly collaborate, they don't just execute better, they communicate better, solve problems faster, and innovate continuously...which is what we want as leaders, isn't it?

Collaboration IS Your Strategy

Innovation rarely fails due to lack of good ideas; it fails due to misalignment, muddy roles, and ineffective collaboration. ***InnoMagination*** isn't just another methodology. It is a straightforward, practical blueprint for embedding collaboration into your company's DNA.

If you're feeling pressure to innovate but struggling to align your teams, don't start from scratch.

Start together.

Collaboration isn't soft stuff. It's strategic clarity. And in today's fast-moving world, it's the only approach that truly works.

Phase 5: OFFER
Aligning InnoMagination with Vision: Ensuring Strategic Coherence

> ***"Innovation is the ability to see change as an opportunity—not a threat. But it must always be anchored to your core strategy."***
>
> — ***A.G. Lafley***

Section Objective: *Reinforce the importance of aligning every* ***InnoMagination*** opportunity *with the organization's Core Essence, ensuring that new ideas build trust, accelerate strategy, and reflect brand, mission, and values with unmistakable clarity.*

InnoMagination without alignment is just noise.

By now, you've heard me say it more than once, but it bears repeating. ***InnoMagination*** isn't chasing the next shiny thing or jumping on the latest trend.

If your new ideas don't deeply align with who your organization is, where you're heading, and how you show up in the world, you're creating distractions, not breakthroughs.

Alignment isn't optional. It is foundational. It's what separates fleeting hype from lasting success and internal chaos from focused momentum.

Why Strategic Alignment Matters So Much

Think of misaligned ***InnoMagination*** as building your dream house on sand. Sure, the curb appeal might impress at first glance, but when storms come, the house is certain to crumble.

When your ***InnoMagination*** opportunities drift from your organization's core, you risk:

- Fragmented focus (teams pulling in opposite directions)
- Confused employees (unclear about the 'why')
- Diluted brand (customers no longer sure who you are)
- Resistance (from the very people whose buy-in you need most)

But when ***InnoMagination*** aligns closely with your organization's *Core Essence*, everything shifts. You create brand clarity, operational synergy, and stakeholder confidence that translates into genuine advocacy.

Your Alignment Filter: *Core Essence*

Remember the *Core Essence Assessment* you completed earlier in this book? It's not just busy work to stick on the shelf. (I was very serious about that!) It really is your strategic litmus test. Let's dust that off and put it to real use now.

Here's exactly how you use it to pressure-test every ***InnoMagination*** opportunity:

Step 1: Reground in Your Core

Before you launch, pitch, or prototype, pause and ask yourself these five critical questions:

1. **Values:** Does this amplify what we truly stand for, or quietly undermine it?

2. **Brand Promise & Perception:** Will customers say, "Well, of course they did this—it's exactly who they are!" or scratch their heads in confusion?

3. **Mission:** Does this move us closer to our purpose, or pull us off course?

4. **Organizational Personality:** Does the opportunity reflect how we uniquely operate, not just what we do?

5. **Strategic Direction:** Does this accelerate our strategic goals, or create unintentional drift?

If even *one* answer feels fuzzy...STOP! Revisit and realign. Clarity now saves pain later.

Step 2: Gut-Check Your Go-To-Market Plan

It's not just about what you build. It's about *how* you bring it to life. Before you move forward, look at your Go-To-Market strategy through this same alignment lens:

- Does this strategy truly feel like us? In tone, approach, execution?

- Will our messaging resonate as authentic, or ring hollow?

- Are our channels and tactics genuinely aligned with how we've chosen to compete?

If the external story doesn't match the internal DNA of your organization, you're setting yourself up for trouble. Authenticity isn't just for people.

Step 3: Enroll the People Who Matter

Alignment isn't just strategy, it's a social contract. You need buy-in from two key groups:

- **Internal Stakeholders:** Can your leaders, teams, and board clearly see how this opportunity connects to the bigger picture? Can they articulate the 'why'?
- **External Stakeholders:** Do your customers, investors, partners, and analysts recognize this as a logical next step?

Your role is to make alignment visible. When people definitively see the connection, they trust your vision—and follow your lead.

Alignment Is a Leadership Metric

Zoom out for a second. Strategic alignment isn't just about smart decision-making. It's critical to how you show up as a leader. Alignment is one proof point of your credibility and readiness for even bigger leadership roles.

Your Reputation Is Built on Alignment

Every ***InnoMagination*** decision you champion either builds or erodes trust. When your ideas consistently reflect your mission and values, you build reputational equity. You'll be known as someone who doesn't just move fast...because you'll move with unmistakable intention.

- Ask: *Am I reinforcing my credibility with every* ***InnoMagination*** *decision or risking it for speed or novelty?*

So You Want to Be "In the Room"? Think Like a Top Executive

Your board doesn't just want cool ideas. They want strategic alignment. When you demonstrate you've pressure-tested your ideas against your organization's core strategy, you're building executive credibility.

- Ask: *Am I owning the strategic narrative or just pitching features and benefits?*

Alignment Reveals Depth

Strategic coherence isn't just about knowing the business. It is a reflection of understanding nuance—how values, brand, mission, and culture intertwine. When your opportunity acknowledges that depth, you're not just a leader, you're the Growth Architect of your organization's future.

- Ask: *If someone audited my decisions, would they see strategic depth or surface-level thinking?*

Alignment Checklist:
Your Strategic Filter for Bold *InnoMagination*

Before you greenlight any ***InnoMagination*** opportunity, ask yourself clearly:

- Does this opportunity reinforce our core values?
- Is it congruent with our customer promise and brand identity?

- Does it genuinely advance our mission?
- Does it reflect how we uniquely operate internally?
- Does it directly move us toward our strategic goals?
- Can I clearly communicate why this fits and why it matters?

If you can't confidently say *"HECK, YEAH!"* to each question, pause and realign.

Remember, *InnoMagination* Without Alignment Is Just Noise

The world is obsessed with what's next. But YOUR real power move is staying anchored in who you truly are. ***InnoMagination*** rooted in strategic alignment doesn't just grab attention, it builds lasting trust, drives momentum, and earns you a meaningful voice in shaping the future.

The key question isn't, "*Can* we do this?"

It's ***"Should we do this...and is it ours to do?"***

Phase 5: OFFER
Metrics of Success: Measuring InnoMagination Effectively

"If you can't measure it, you can't improve it."

— Peter Drucker

Section Objective: *Establish how to measure* ***InnoMagination*** opportunities *through strategically aligned, organization-relevant KPIs, ensuring* ***InnoMagination*** *efforts clearly demonstrate business impact, build credibility, and drive outcomes the business already values.*

At the end of the day, the question you must answer isn't just "Did we build something new?" It's "Did it move the business forward in a measurable, strategic way?"

That's where ***InnoMagination*** will help you prove you aren't just doing innovation for innovation's sake. You are innovating on purpose. You're aligned to your organization's *Core Essence* and measuring against what already matters to the business.

Measurement Must Reflect Strategy—Not Reinvent It

We don't need to invent new metrics to prove ***InnoMagination*** works. In fact, doing so can backfire. If your success metrics aren't tied to what the C-suite and board already track, your ***InnoMagination*** opportunity risks becoming an irrelevant, siloed experiment instead of a strategic growth lever.

InnoMagination efforts must plug directly into the KPIs that already define success across the organization. That's how you earn credibility, justify investment, and prove that ***InnoMagination*** isn't a side hustle; it's a driver of growth and transformation.

Why Baselines Matter: Before-and-After Storytelling

Every ***InnoMagination*** effort should tell a clear, compelling "then-and-now" story.

Before you launch anything, establish your baseline metrics. Get clear on where you are so you can track where you're going. Then, after execution, revisit those same metrics regularly and consistently to show tangible impact.

Whether you're launching a new customer experience, repositioning the brand, or opening a new market, it's the delta that matters. ***Did you move the needle?***

Strategic Metrics That Matter

Here are some of the most powerful, enterprise-anchored metrics to measure ***InnoMagination*** success through the ***InnoMagination*** lens. These aren't vanity metrics. They're the language that prove your effectiveness.

- **Revenue Growth**
  Are we unlocking new revenue streams, accelerating sales cycles, or expanding into higher-margin segments?

- **Return on Marketing Investment (ROMI)**

Are we generating better returns on our marketing spend through more resonant positioning, storytelling, or customer experiences?

- **Customer Acquisition Cost (CAC)**
  Is our ***InnoMagination*** opportunity making it easier, faster, or cheaper to attract our ideal customer?

- **Market Share**
  Are we gaining ground relative to competitors in key segments or markets?

- **Brand Equity**
  Is our brand more valuable? Is this value reflected in awareness, preference, and willingness to pay?

- **Brand Positioning & Reputation**
  How has our perception shifted? Are we seen as more innovative, trustworthy, or relevant?

- **Customer Retention & Renewals**
  Are we driving loyalty through better experiences, deeper relationships, or increased value delivery?

- **Customer Satisfaction & Engagement (as measured by CSAT, NPS, etc.)**
  Are our customers more satisfied, vocal, and engaged as a result of this ***InnoMagination*** opportunity?

The Real Test: Alignment Over Novelty

Measuring ***InnoMagination*** is not about showcasing how "new" or "cool" something is. You must prove it's aligned. Remember, strategic alignment is the multiplier. When ***InnoMagination*** is clearly fueling the organization's most critical goals, it earns the right to scale.

So before you design your metrics dashboard to measure anything, ask:

- Does this ***InnoMagination*** effort support a core business priority?
- Does it solve a real problem for a real customer?
- Can we link it to a measurable business outcome already being tracked?

If the answer is yes, that's great. You're building with integrity. If not, pause. Recalibrate. Realign before you launch.

Speak the Language of the Business

InnoMagination leaders don't just build. **They translate.** They connect the dots between creativity and commerce, between ideas and impact.

The most effective Growth leaders don't ask for permission to innovate. They show results in metrics the business already values. They don't just introduce new concepts, they make those concepts measurable, scalable, and strategically undeniable.

That's how you build trust and earn investment. And that's how you turn ***InnoMagination*** into an engine of long-term growth.

Stop! This is a good time to hold a mini-Collaboration check with just your Collaboration team.

Confirm you are on track via the *Alignment Checklist* (above), then ensure you've selected the best metrics based on the KPIs of your organization.

This step is essential. You can totally blow up all your good work at this point if either your offer idea or your metrics are misaligned.

Phase 5: OFFER
Building An Effective Business Case

> ***"A good idea without a compelling business case is like an airplane without wings—it won't get off the ground." — Attributed to Sir Richard Branson***

Section Objective: *Equip leaders with a clear, enterprise-ready structure for building a compelling business case that aligns* ***InnoMagination*** *with strategy, quantifies value, manages risk, and earns executive buy-in to move from vision to execution.*

If you can't make your business case, you can't make the business move.

InnoMagination without execution is a dream. ***InnoMagination*** without a business case is a dead end. It doesn't matter how brilliant your idea is, if you can't clearly demonstrate how it will move the business forward, you won't get the buy-in, resources, or runway to make it real. And here's the key: Your business case isn't just a formality. It's how you demonstrate that your ***InnoMagination*** opportunity isn't just bold; it's viable, valuable, and aligned with the organization's strategic direction. Let's break down how to build one that earns attention and approval.

The Purpose of a Business Case: From Idea to Investment

The business case is how you translate the results of your work through the ***InnoMagination*** process into business logic. It's where your vision meets viability.

At its most basic level, a business case must answer the following:

- What are we doing?
- Why now?
- What's the upside (ROI)?
- What are the risks?
- How much will it cost?
- How long will it take?
- Who's involved?
- What does success look like?

- How does it align with where we're already going?

Remember, this isn't innovation for grins and giggles. It's innovation *on purpose*, with a clear roadmap, strategic fit, and measurable return. You must be able to articulate your proposal to get the buy-in and resources to execute it.

Start With Strategy: Align Before You Ask

As we discussed previously, before you build your case, you must align with the organization's existing priorities. Don't create a parallel narrative. Plug into the one that's already in motion.

Ask yourself:

- What are the CEO's top three priorities this year?
- What metrics are the board watching most closely?
- Where is the organization already investing heavily?
- What risks are being actively managed right now?

Your business case should feel like the next right move, not a departure from organizational strategy. If it doesn't ladder up to enterprise goals—it won't get funded and it may be purposely blocked or railroaded.

First Comes Go-To-Market (GTM), Then Comes the Business Case

Before you start crunching numbers or building slides, build your Go-To-Market hypothesis. You need to know how this ***InnoMagination*** effort will show up in the world, how it will generate revenue or impact, and what it will take to get there.

Your GTM[2] strategy gives your business case teeth. It informs:

- Revenue models
- Customer acquisition costs
- Operational dependencies
- Resource allocation
- Launch timelines

If your GTM plan isn't clear, your business case will be full of assumptions...and executives don't fund assumptions.

The Critical Components of a High-Trust Business Case

Now let's get into the structure. Here's what decision-makers expect to see, and what you must prepare to answer with clarity and confidence.

1. Executive Summary & Recommendation

This is your elevator pitch in writing.

What are you proposing? Why is it important? What do you need? Offer a concise recommendation right up front.

Tip: Treat this like a boardroom headline. Be bold, specific, and outcome-driven.

---

2. Check out Sangram Vajre's *Move: The 4-Question Go-To-Market Framework*[56] for excellent advice on developing an end-to-end GTM strategy across all the departments required to get a product to market effectively.

2. Project Definition

Define the scope, objectives, and boundaries of the initiative.
What are you building, improving, or launching? What's in scope and what's not?

3. Problem Statement

Frame the pain point, opportunity, or business gap.
Why is this a problem worth solving now? Use real data, customer and market insights, or market trends to anchor urgency.

4. Context

Provide the strategic and market backdrop.
What's happening internally or externally that creates the need—or the opportunity—for this effort?

Link to enterprise strategy, competitor moves, customer expectations, or macro shifts.

5. Solution Options

Show that you've explored multiple paths.

Present 2–3 potential solutions (including the "do nothing" option and the potential implications) and explain why your recommended approach is the best path forward.

Tip: This builds trust across the C-suite and board. Prove you're not emotionally attached, you're analytically sound.

6. Success Criteria

Define how you'll measure success.
What KPIs will you track? What does success look like at 30, 60, 90, and 180 days post-launch?

Tie these directly to enterprise metrics like:

- Revenue growth
- Return on marketing investment
- Market share
- Brand equity
- Brand positioning and reputation
- Customer retention & renewals
- Customer satisfaction
- Operational efficiency

7. Cost-Benefit Analysis

This is where the math matters.

Estimate the total investment required (time, people, money, tech) and quantify the anticipated return.

Include:

- ROI (Return on Investment)
- Payback period
- Potential cost savings or avoidance
- Long-term upside

Tip: Be conservative, but confident. Show your work, and be ready to defend your assumptions.

8. Risk Assessment

Map out potential risks and how you'll mitigate them.

From market volatility to internal resistance, *be honest* about what could go wrong and what contingencies you've built in.

This is a good time to discuss opportunity cost. What can't you do or what will the organization forfeit if you pursue this opportunity?

Whatever you do, do NOT say that there are no risks or that you do not anticipate any! There are always some risks, no matter how small. Identify them and create a mitigation plan.

This shows maturity, not weakness. Risk-aware leaders are trusted leaders.

9. Execution Plan (GTM Strategy)

Lay out your launch and delivery plan. *Who does what, by when, using which resources?*

Include timeline, milestones, and ownership.

This is where you show you're not just an idea person. You're a leader who operationalizes vision.

The GTM Strategy: Your Operational Blueprint

Your GTM strategy isn't just a marketing plan. It's much more than that. It's the *cross-functional* operating model that brings your ***InnoMagination*** opportunity to market and ensures it sticks.

This is where most business cases fall apart, because the execution plan is vague, siloed (e.g., just focusing on Marketing and Sales), or incomplete.

Your GTM strategy <u>must</u> coordinate across:

- **Marketing**: Messaging, content, campaigns, positioning
- **Sales Enablement**: Tools, training, competitive intel
- **Sales & Pre-Sales**: Prospecting, demos, closing
- **Customer Success & Support**: Onboarding, retention, advocacy
- **Revenue Operations**: Forecasting, pipeline, performance
- **Billing & Finance**: Pricing, packaging, billing logic, contract management
- **Change Management & Communications**: Internal rollout, alignment
- **Governance & Leadership**: Executive oversight and accountability

Your GTM strategy <u>must</u> answer:

- Who are we selling to? (Ideal customer profile, market segments, geographies)
- What are we selling? (Product/service definition and value prop)
- Why do they need it? (Problem-solution fit)

- Where can we reach them? (Channels, platforms, partnerships)
- How do we Go-To-Market? (Tactics, plays, timing)
- When should we launch? (Market readiness, internal alignment)
- How will we measure success? (KPIs, feedback loops, learning cycles, plans to scale)

After you complete preparation of the business case, it's time to hold your executive briefing and present the business case and GTM plan. Pre-plan and identify all the questions and objections you are likely to encounter and develop data-backed responses.

Know your numbers and the data inside and out.

Remember how I said the Collaboration Checks would help you later? They serve as the pre-framing to the business case. In other words, your business case should be the logical extension of the five-phase journey you've been leading these key stakeholders through.

The opportunity you present will most certainly be creative and compelling but the process must make strategic, aligned, low-risk sense to data-driven executives.

Business Cases Are How *InnoMagination* Gets Funded

Bold ideas don't get funded. Believable plans do.

When you build a business case that aligns with strategy, speaks the language of the business, and demonstrates thoughtful execution, you earn the right to move ***InnoMagination*** from the whiteboard to the real world.

This is how you turn "I've got an idea" into "We're building this next quarter."

TEN

READY, SET, INNOVATE: IMPLEMENTING INNOMAGINATION

"Ideas are easy. Implementation is hard."

— Guy Kawasaki

Chapter Objective: *Provide a practical roadmap for implementing* ***InnoMagination™*** *within existing organizational structures, demonstrating how to activate* ***InnoMagination*** *through cross-functional collaboration, flexible resourcing, and phased execution without disrupting core operations.*

You don't need more bandwidth to innovate. You need a better blueprint.

You might be thinking, ***InnoMagination*** feels like a luxury...something to get to after the fires are out, the quarter is closed, and the team bandwidth magically appears.

Really?? You and I both know, that is never going to happen (and if it miraculously did, you'd take a much needed vacation!). Waiting for the "right time" to innovate is a strategic delay tactic. And delay, in today's market, is a risk you can't afford.

The good news is you don't need to overhaul your organization to get moving. ***InnoMagination*** is designed to work with your existing structure, not against it. It meets you where you are and helps you build momentum without breaking your current operations.

Let's talk about how to get started—without disruption—and how to scale with confidence.

InnoMagination Isn't a Department. It's a Distributed Capability.

One of the biggest misconceptions in the C-suite is that innovation should sit in a silo, owned by a single team, lab, or executive. But ***InnoMagination***? It's distributed. Democratized, really. It requires participation, ownership, and energy from both the top and the bottom of the organization.

Leaders must do two things:

1. Create the conditions for ***InnoMagination*** to emerge
2. Empower teams with both the agency and capacity to act on the ideas they generate

This isn't just giving permission. It's resourcing ***InnoMagination***, prioritizing it, and integrating it into the flow of business.

Three Ways to Execute Without Overload

You don't need to hire a new team or launch a special office to bring **InnoMagination** to life. However, it is one thing to theoretically *understand* the steps; *doing* them is another.

Fortunately, you don't have to figure it out alone.

You've got the belief. Now let us bring the structure, momentum, and strategic firepower to move it forward, without burning out your team.

Here are three ways to get started—including one where **we guide you every step of the way.**

1. Engage an *InnoMagination* Advisor (That's Us)

If your team is stretched thin or unsure where to begin, **we'll run the full *InnoMagination* process for you.**

We interact with your team through every phase as we develop a fully articulated, ready-to-sell business case and Go-To-Market strategy.

You get clarity, alignment, and a compelling plan your leadership team can confidently approve.

We don't just advise—we facilitate, synthesize, and deliver the strategic output.

You stay focused on your business. We help you unlock the next big growth opportunity already inside it.

2. Activate Your In-House Marketing Function

Already have a strong strategic Marketing team? Perfect. They're already positioned at the intersection of insight, product, and brand.

We can help them lead a cross-functional ***InnoMagination*** initiative with confidence, clarity, and executive alignment.

We'll give them the framework and help them drive it.

3. Partner with a Strategic Agency

If you're already working with an external marketing agency, we can collaborate with them to support the strategy.

We'll bring the big-picture thinking and ***InnoMagination*** DNA—they'll execute the campaigns, assets, and activation.

TIP: Just make sure they're wired for growth, not just production.

Bottom Line:

If you're thinking, "I love this framework, but I need help making it real..."

Know that you're not alone.

Let us walk with you. We'll help you translate insight into action—step by step, team by team.

You don't need more hustle. You need a strategic partner.

That's who we are.

The *InnoMagination* Implementation Path

Regardless of how you resource it, the path to implementation follows the same strategic progression. Here's how ***InnoMagination*** moves seamlessly from idea to market impact:

1. Complete the *InnoMagination* assessment process

Conduct the full five-phase assessment:

- **IDENTITY:** Clarify your *Core Essence* and uncover internal assets.
- **LANDSCAPE:** Research market trends, customer behaviors, and competitive dynamics.
- **MARKETPLACE:** Identify market gaps and unmet customer needs.
- **PURSUIT:** Evaluate and prioritize opportunities strategically.
- **OFFER:** Architect a clear, compelling offer; develop your Go-To-Market (GTM) strategy and create an executive-facing business case.

2. Test & Refine

With your offer clearly defined, experiment and pilot it at a manageable scale. Gather real-world data, observe customer behaviors, refine your value proposition, and sharpen your messaging before full-scale launch.

3. Launch

After successfully piloting and refining the offer, execute your full-scale market launch. Ensure internal alignment, direct, transparent communication, and strategic execution supported by validated insights.

4. Measure, Iterate & Scale

Post-launch, continuously track market performance, customer feedback, and operational data. Iterate quickly, adjusting positioning, optimizing messaging, and strengthening alignment. Use these insights to scale effectively and feed continuous improvement into future ***InnoMagination*** cycles.

Scaling Looks Like This

Scaling isn't just about doing more. It's taking what you have learned along the way and doing it smarter and more efficiently.

Once your ***InnoMagination***-led initiative is in motion, scaling means:

- Making data-driven adjustments to your messaging, experience, or product features.
- Refining your market positioning using real insights from customers and frontline teams.
- Expanding your partnerships to reach new audiences or add new capabilities.
- Increasing efforts on what's working, and pivoting quickly away from what's not.

Continue to evaluate your initiative quarterly for potential ways to improve the offering. You may hit upon a fresh path to ***InnoMaginate*** and build on it for even more growth in the future.

Whether you start with one team, one pilot, or one product line, the key is to start. Give your people the structure, support, and space to innovate within the flow of business, not outside of it.

The companies that win in the next decade won't be the ones who had the best ideas. They'll be the ones who knew how to bring them to life, without waiting for perfect conditions.

Reflection Prompts for Leaders

Use these prompts to turn insight into action:

- Where could we embed ***InnoMagination*** into existing projects or teams without adding new overhead?
- Which internal functions or external partners are best positioned to lead early implementation?
- Are we giving our teams both the permission and the capacity to innovate or just lip service?

ELEVEN

BUILDING A CULTURE OF INNOMAGINATION

"The greatest danger in times of turbulence is not the turbulence—it is to act with yesterday's logic."

— Peter Drucker

Chapter Objective: *Provide Growth leaders with actionable strategies to break organizational inertia by shifting culture, modeling leadership behaviors, embedding **InnoMagination**™ into existing systems, and sustaining momentum through clarity, alignment, and intentional change.*

When 'business as usual' starts sabotaging your next breakthrough, it's not just time for a new playbook. It's time to change the game.

Organizational Inertia is the Silent Killer of Innovation.
It's not that your team lacks ideas. Or that leadership doesn't care. It's that the gravitational pull of the *status quo* is stronger than the momentum of what's next.

And that's exactly where the ***Legacy Lock Contradiction*** shows up again:

> ***"Organizations want innovation, but their systems, culture, and incentives are perfectly designed to protect what already exists."***

So how do you break the cycle? How do you unstick a stuck organization, especially when you're already running lean, under pressure, and managing change fatigue?

The answer starts at the top, but it's not just there.

Innovation doesn't usually fail because of bad ideas. It often fails because of invisible resistance—the kind that hides in cultural norms, outdated processes, and leadership habits too ingrained to notice.

And it's not that your people aren't smart, creative, or willing. It's that the system they operate in rewards predictability over possibility. That system must be challenged...and that starts with you.

A Cultural Shift Isn't Optional. It's the Engine.

InnoMagination isn't a tactic. It's a culture.

You can't implement ***InnoMagination***—or any innovation strategy for that matter—on top of a culture that punishes risk, avoids change, or idolizes "what's always worked."

Cultural transformation doesn't require a rebrand or 12 months of workshops. It requires visible leadership behavior that signals a new standard.

Here's what that looks like:

- Rewarding learning, not just outcomes
- Normalizing iteration instead of expecting perfection
- Creating psychological safety for bold ideas to surface
- Resourcing ***InnoMagination*** with time, talent, and trust

When your people see that ***InnoMagination*** isn't just a buzzword or the latest top-down management fad *du jour*, but rather a behavior you encourage and expect, they'll start to move *with* you.

InnoMagination Only Moves at the Speed of Belief

You cannot plug ***InnoMagination*** into a culture built for control and consistency.

You have to reshape the system from the inside out.

That doesn't mean tearing everything down. It does mean rewiring how people behave, what gets rewarded, and how decisions get made.

The shift starts with four visible signals:

1. **Psychological safety**: Risk-taking isn't punished; it's expected.
2. **Permission to challenge norms:** "That's how we've always done it" is not a valid excuse.
3. **Learning velocity > perfection**: Iteration is the goal, not flawless execution.
4. **Recognition for progress**: Celebrate forward movement, not just moonshots.

When your culture rewards curiosity, ownership, and bold thinking, ***InnoMagination*** moves from aspiration to operating system.

Leadership Commitment is the Non-Negotiable Price of Progress
Here's the thing. You can't delegate transformation. ***InnoMagination*** initiatives die when leaders treat them like side projects instead of strategic imperatives.

What commitment looks like in practice (and yes, this is about to get uncomfortable!):

- Showing up to ***InnoMagination*** reviews with the same energy as board meetings
- Making ***InnoMagination*** goals part of executive scorecards
- Sponsoring pilots, not just approving them.[1]
- Allocating real budget (not scraps) for experimentation
- Protecting time to think, test, and iterate, even when other fires are burning and the quarter's resources get tight
- Publicly celebrating progress, not just outcomes
- Holding other leaders accountable for creating ***InnoMagination***-friendly, collaborative environments

---

1. *Note: Sponsoring is actively championing the vision, removing obstacles, advocating across teams, and putting your personal credibility on the line to ensure success. A true sponsor doesn't just approve* ***InnoMagination****. They own it, protect it, and clear the path for it.*

Why? Because your people take their cues from you. If you're indifferent, they'll disengage. If you model it, they'll follow. You don't have to lead every project, but you do have to lead the charge.

Six Strategies to Break Inertia and Build Momentum

You don't have to solve everything at once to get started. The following strategies will help you shift energy from stuck to in-motion, without disrupting operations.

1. Start with a Strategic Wedge

Don't try to transform the whole organization. Start with one team, one customer segment, or one product line. Choose something strategically significant but operationally manageable and make it your proving ground.

Begin where you have:

- Obvious pain or opportunity
- Executive sponsorship
- Willing cross-functional partners

This becomes your proof of concept and your internal case study for what's possible when the system flexes.

2. Complete an Organizational Inertia Audit

Run an audit to identify exactly where and why momentum is stalling:

- Is it leadership drift?
- Fear of failure?

- Cultural drag?
- Operational misalignment?
- Communication breakdown?

Once you know the root cause, you can target your response. No more guessing or generic solutions.

Tip: Use the audit quarterly to keep momentum from quietly slipping.

3. Use the *InnoMagination* Framework to Create Clarity

Often, inertia isn't resistance or rebellion, it's confusion. People may just lack understanding of where you are going and what they need to do. You may need to communicate the vision and the plan more clearly. Use the framework to create alignment around your:

- *Core Essence*
- GTM strategy
- Success metrics
- Business case

When teams know why ***InnoMagination*** matters and how and where to move, they move faster.

4. Integrate, Don't Add

I've said it before, but it bears repeating—Don't add "One. More. Thing!"

While very effective, you don't necessarily need to create a separate "***InnoMagination*** lane." You can accomplish a similar effect by embedding ***InnoMagination*** into existing rhythms and workflows:

- Use your current planning cycles to identify ***InnoMagination*** priorities and experimentation opportunities
- Incorporate ***InnoMagination*** KPIs into performance reviews and OKRs
- Build business case reviews into standing leadership meetings
- Assign ***InnoMagination*** roles to cross-functional team leads, not just "***InnoMagination*** teams"

This keeps ***InnoMagination*** in the flow of business, not siloed on the side. It should become part of your innovation culture.

5. Apply Change Management with Precision

Pull through the strategies we discussed earlier:

- Over-communicate early and often, especially the "why" behind the shift
- Create visible wins to build belief in the process
- Equip middle managers with tools to support, not stall
- Involve cross-functional champions to multiply momentum
- Build feedback loops so people feel heard, not steamrolled

Although it may *feel* like you are managing resistance, you really aren't. You're building your necessary momentum.

6. Model the Behavior. Publicly.

Momentum isn't maintained through policy. It is sustained through modeling. If you want your teams to act differently, you have to lead differently.

- Ask better questions ("What did we learn?" vs. "Did it work?")
- Rewarding effort, not just outcomes
- Celebrate smart risks
- Admit what they're learning
- Sponsor ***InnoMagination*** with real resources
- Protect time and space for ***InnoMagination***, not just approve it

Leadership modeling is the fastest way to shift energy in an organization.

How to Sustain Momentum After You Break Through

Getting started is hard. Staying unstuck is harder. Here's how to keep the flywheel turning once it's in motion:

- Measure what matters. Go beyond activity and measure impact. Track ROI, customer impact, customer behavior changes, culture shifts, and team engagement, not just project completion.
- Create a storytelling rhythm. Share wins, learnings, and pivots across the organization early and often. Build belief and reinforce your success.
- Feed the loop. Every ***InnoMagination*** cycle should inform the

next. Use data, feedback, and learnings to evolve continuously.

- Celebrate progress, not just perfection. Momentum compounds when people feel seen and successful.
- Reinforce alignment. Anchor back to *Core Essence*. Use your strategic compass to keep ***InnoMagination*** aligned and on-message.
- Scale what works. Once a pilot proves out, apply the model elsewhere with intentionality.
- Refresh your leadership commitment. Don't assume one round of support is enough. Keep showing up and communicate clearly and constantly.

Last Thoughts: You're Not Stuck. You're Ready.

Inertia isn't a sign that ***InnoMagination*** won't work. It's actually proof that your systems are doing exactly what they were designed to do—protect the past.

But YOUR job isn't to preserve the past. It's to build the future and that starts by breaking the cycle.

Use the tools. Lead the shift. Create the space.

The only thing standing between you and a culture of ***InnoMagination*** is the courage to move.

Reflection Prompts for Leaders

Use these prompts to turn insight into action:

- Have I created visible signals that ***InnoMagination*** is a priority and not a project?
- What's one behavior I can model this week to reinforce our ***InnoMagination*** culture?
- Where is inertia surfacing in our current initiatives? What's my next move to address it?
- What current behaviors, systems, or beliefs in our organization are reinforcing the *status quo*?
- Where could we apply a strategic wedge to prove what's possible?
- Am I modeling the mindset and commitment I'm asking others to adopt?

TWELVE

INNOVATING WHEN RESOURCES ARE TIGHT

"Constraints drive creativity. Limitations force you to think differently."

—Jack Dorsey

Chapter Objective: *Empower leaders to innovate strategically within resource-constrained environments by focusing on clarity, alignment, and precision—proving that momentum, creativity, and impact are possible even without big budgets or large teams.*

You don't need more to DO more. You just need to do the RIGHT things BETTER.

Sure, innovation *sounds* exciting until you're staring at a flat budget, a lean team, and a long list of competing priorities. For many Marketing leaders, the biggest barrier to driving meaningful innovation isn't lack of vision. It is lack of resources.

But in reality, resource constraints don't kill innovation, misalignment does.

When strategy, team energy, and execution aren't working in concert, even the best-funded initiatives stall. But when they're aligned, even scrappy efforts can punch above their weight.

InnoMagination was designed for this exact moment.

You don't need more resources. You need clearer choices.

Some of the most powerful innovations in history weren't born from massive budgets or bloated teams. They were hatched from constraints that forced clarity.

InnoMagination gives you that clarity. It helps you:

- Focus on what matters most
- Align limited resources toward maximum-leverage opportunities
- Empower teams to take action without waiting for "perfect conditions"

InnoMagination isn't a luxury. It's a discipline and discipline thrives under pressure.

Three Principles for Innovating When Resources Are Tight

1. Do Less, But With Greater Precision

When budget and bandwidth are limited, focus is your greatest asset.

Instead of spreading effort across multiple ideas or priorities, concentrate on one or two high-leverage opportunities that:

- Align clearly with your *Core Essence*
- Have strong customer pull or urgency

- Can deliver measurable ROI quickly

Use the ***InnoMagination*** framework to evaluate where you get the most strategic and emotional return. Then intensify your efforts.

Constraint is a form of prioritization. A gift really. Use it as your superpower.

2. Empower Cross-Functional Teams to Lead the Charge
You don't need to build new teams. You simply need to unleash the potential within the ones you already have.

Form small, empowered, cross-functional pods anchored in a shared goal. Give them:

- Clear guardrails
- Strategic context
- Permission to make decisions
- A direct line to leadership for unblocking obstacles

This creates micro-momentum, and when you link those wins together, they become powerful points of progress.

When resources are tight, autonomy and trust expand capacity.

3. Reframe Constraints as Creative Catalysts
InnoMagination thrives on questions like:

- "What could we do with what we already have?"
- "What if we partnered instead of building?"

- "How could we test this without scaling it first?"

Encourage teams to prototype, pilot, and iterate using existing tools, channels, and customer touchpoints.

Don't cut corners. *Build smarter.*

Lean into low-cost experiments that generate high-value insights.

Six Practical Moves to Sustain *InnoMagination* Momentum on a Lean Budget

1. Use the GTM Plan as a Capacity Filter

Go lean. Prioritize only the tactics that are essential to your launch hypothesis. Drop the rest. You can always revisit them after you prove your hypothesis and it's time to scale.

2. Leverage Existing Platforms & Tools

Don't buy new tech. Use what you have in new ways. By some estimates, most organizations are only using 60% of their existing tools' capabilities.[57] Someone is managing your techstack. Find out who it is, get close to them, discover what tools are available, and gain access to what you need.

3. Tap Internal Talent Creatively

Look for hidden innovators. Identify people who are under-utilized, undervalued, or hungry to lead something new or take on a side project. (You might have identified these secret innovators during your Inventory Audit process.)

4. Co-Create with Customers

Involve your best customers in early-stage ideation or testing. It builds loyalty and saves development cycles.

5. Borrow Resources Through Strategic Partnerships

Find adjacent companies, platforms, or service providers that can co-create, co-brand, or co-deliver.

6. Celebrate and Share Early Wins

Energy is a resource. And recognition generates more of it. Share progress loudly and often.

Keeping Your Team Motivated in Lean Times

It's easy for teams to disengage when they feel stretched and unsupported. Here's how to keep them energized, even when resources are tight:

- **Reinforce purpose.** Remind them why this specific ***InnoMagination*** opportunity matters to the business and to the customer.

- **Create micro-wins.** Set short-term goals that show movement and progress.

- **Make space for ALL voices.** Involve them in decision-making. Invite their ideas. Respond to their feedback.

- **Recognize effort.** In a resource-constrained environment, the work ethic behind ***InnoMagination*** matters as much as results.

- **Connect their effort to impact.** Show them how their work is influencing change, even in small ways.

Motivation doesn't come from money. It comes from meaning, movement, and momentum.

Last Thoughts: Constraint Is a Canvas

InnoMagination wasn't built for perfect conditions. It was built for real leaders in real companies doing bold work with limited resources (i.e., today's environment).

When you apply its principles—clarity, alignment, strategy, and execution—you stop waiting for more and start doing more with what you've already got.

InnoMagination isn't about having everything you want. It's about knowing exactly what to do with what you already have.

Reflection Prompts for Leaders

Use these prompts to turn insight into action:

- Where are we mistaking lack of resources for lack of possibility?
- How can we better leverage the teams, tools, and trust we already have?
- What's one high-leverage bet we can make in the next 30 days with the resources available to us right now?

THIRTEEN

AVOIDING PITFALLS IN INNOMAGINATING

"Learn from the mistakes of others. You can't live long enough to make them all yourself."

— Eleanor Roosevelt

Chapter Objective: *Identify and address the top pitfalls leaders face when* ***InnoMaginating*** *existing products—offering actionable strategies to avoid misalignment, overengineering, and missed opportunities while reinforcing* ***InnoMagination***^{TM} *as a continuous, cross-functional discipline.*

For Marketing and Growth leaders, the concept of innovating an existing product or service can feel deceptively simple. You know the market. You've got traction. You've already done the hard part, right?

Not quite.

Truthfully, innovating what already exists can be more complex, more political, and more emotionally charged than launching something new. You're not just building, you're 'unbalancing' what's already 'working.' And that means facing resistance, legacy constraints, and the potential risk of making things worse if you're not careful.

Let's break down the most common traps leaders fall into and how to navigate around them with precision.

The Top 10 Pitfalls of *InnoMagination*:

1. Innovating in isolation
2. Overcorrecting instead of iterating
3. Misalignment with brand and strategy
4. Feature creep masquerading as innovation
5. Undervaluing internal impact
6. Not measuring the right things
7. Ignoring ecosystem interdependencies
8. Waiting for "perfect" before shipping
9. Failing to reposition the offering
10. Treating ***InnoMagination*** as a one-time event

Pitfall #1: *InnoMaginating* in Isolation
The Trap: Teams *InnoMaginate* in silos, disconnected from customer feedback, frontline insights, or strategic direction.

When you try to ***InnoMaginate*** a product without involving the people closest to the problem—your customers, your Customer Success reps, your Sales teams—you miss the nuances that drive real value.

Here's What To Do Instead:

Use the ***InnoMagination*** framework to ground your decisions in:

- Your *Core Essence*
- Real customer pain points
- Strategic priorities

Co-create with the people who use, sell, or support the product every day. ***InnoMagination*** shouldn't be a surprise. It should feel inevitable.

Pitfall #2: Over-correcting Instead of Iterating
The Trap: In trying to make a big leap, teams throw out what's working and overbuild a new experience that confuses or alienates users.

This is especially common when a product has been stable for years and leaders want to "make it fresh." But dramatic pivots without clear rationale or testing for feedback can erode customer trust—and internal confidence.

Here's What To Do Instead:

- Focus on layered ***InnoMagination***. Look for small, strategic shifts that build on strengths
- Use test & refine loops before launching anything at scale
- Clearly communicate why changes are being made, and how they improve the experience or value

Pitfall #3: Misalignment with Brand and Strategy
The Trap: *InnoMagination* becomes disconnected from the brand promise or strategic direction, creating confusion in the market.

InnoMagination that dilutes your core brand perception—or sends mixed signals to customers—also erodes trust, even if the feature is good.

Here's What To Do Instead:

- Revisit your *Core Essence Assessment*
- Ask: *Does this* ***InnoMagination*** *effort reinforce our brand promise?*
- Check alignment with your current Go-To-Market strategy and long-term positioning

Your ***InnoMagination*** should feel like an evolution, not a departure.

Pitfall #4: Feature Creep Masquerading as *InnoMagination*
The Trap: Teams mistake adding more features for adding more value.

This is one of the most common forms of innovation theater. It looks like progress, but it often makes the product more complex, harder to use, and more expensive to maintain.

Here's What To Do Instead:

- Focus on *clarity of value*, not volume of features
- Use customer journey mapping to identify opportunities where ***InnoMagination*** could drive impact

- Prioritize simplification over expansion, especially in mature products

Pitfall #5: Undervaluing the Internal Impact
The Trap: Leaders focus only on the customer-facing change and neglect the internal shifts required to support it.

Every ***InnoMagination*** effort has ripple effects across:

- Sales Enablement processes and materials
- Support training
- Customer Success workflows
- Billing or packaging logic

Here's What To Do Instead:

- Involve internal teams early in the ***InnoMagination*** process
- Build a GTM Execution Plan that includes Enablement, Support, and RevOps
- Use change management strategies to align, equip, and enroll the people who'll carry the product forward

Pitfall #6: Not Measuring the Right Things
The Trap: Success is measured by launch velocity or usage metrics alone—not by strategic outcomes or customer impact.

It's easy to track downloads, logins, time in-app, or heaven forbid—vanity metrics (likes, shares, pageviews, and number of followers). It's harder—but more valuable—to track:

- Expansion revenue
- Retention
- Brand perception shifts
- Marketshare
- Strategic positioning gains

Here's What To Do Instead:

- Define specific success criteria at the start
- Align to existing enterprise metrics wherever possible
- Use the Strategic Alignment Checklist to ensure your ***InnoMagination*** effort is pulling in the right direction

Pitfall #7: Ignoring Ecosystem Interdependencies
The Trap: Leaders treat *InnoMagination* as an isolated decision, not realizing how deeply their offering is embedded in a broader ecosystem.

Like impacts that ripple through a broken supply chain, your product and market ecosystem is complex and can have lasting knock-on effects if not properly managed. When you change one part of the experience—pricing, packaging, integrations, delivery—you affect everything from partner relationships to operational workflows to fulfillment.

Here's What To Do Instead:

- Map the entire value chain and ecosystem around the product

- Consider impacts on partners, platforms, and integrations
- Bring ecosystem stakeholders into the planning process early

Pitfall #8: Waiting for "Perfect" Before Shipping
The Trap: Teams over-polish, over-plan, or over-engineer the *InnoMagination effort,* often delaying launch and losing momentum.

This is usually driven by fear: fear of failure, fear of stakeholder judgment, fear of customer feedback. The result? Missed windows, internal fatigue, and diluted urgency.

Here's What To Do Instead:

- Use the *Test & Refine* step from the ***InnoMagination*** **Implementation Path** (Chapter 9)
- Launch a pilot or beta to a small segment of users
- Treat launch as the beginning of learning, not the end of development

Progress over perfection. Every. Single. Time.

Pitfall #9: Failing to Reposition the Offering
The Trap: Teams innovate the product but keep the same messaging, pricing, or positioning, so customers don't see the value.

You can't assume customers will "just get it." If the story doesn't change, the perception won't either, no matter how great the update is.

Here's What To Do Instead:

- Revisit the positioning strategy as part of your GTM plan
- Update messaging to reflect the evolved value proposition
- Train and enable Sales, Marketing, and Customer Success teams to tell the new story

Pitfall #10: Treating *InnoMagination* as a One-Time Event
The Trap: Once the updated product is launched, the team moves on, without building a loop for learning, iteration, and continuous improvement.

Post-launch is where the real opportunity begins. If you stop here, you miss valuable insights and risk stagnation all over again.

Here's What To Do Instead:

- Build a *Measure & Iterate* loop into your GTM execution
- Set checkpoints at 30/60/90 days post-launch
- Use customer feedback, usage data, and internal insights to refine and expand

Last Thoughts: *InnoMagination* Isn't a Feature—It's a Discipline
When you're innovating an existing product, you're playing on a live stage. Customers are watching. Competitors are watching. Your own teams are watching.

You can't just be fast. You must also be focused, aligned, and intentional.

Use the ***InnoMagination*** framework to avoid the noise, cut through the traps, and deliver ***InnoMagination*** efforts that your customers feel, your teams believe in, and your business benefits from.

When you get it right, innovating what already exists could become the most powerful growth lever you have.

Reflection Prompts for Leaders

Use these prompts to turn insight into action:

- Are we adding features or solving real problems?
- Is our ***InnoMagination*** opportunity aligned with our brand promise and strategic direction?
- Have we equipped our internal teams to support and scale this?
- Are we measuring success in a way that reflects real business impact?

FOURTEEN

AI WON'T REPLACE STRATEGY: HOW TO USE IT TO ACCELERATE INNOMAGINATION

"Technology is nothing. What's important is that you have faith in people, that they're basically good and smart, and if you give them tools, they'll do wonderful things with them."

— Steve Jobs

Chapter Objective: *Clarify the role of AI as a powerful enabler (not a replacement) for strategic* ***InnoMagination™****, showing leaders how to leverage AI within the InnoMagination framework to accelerate insight, ideation, and execution while remaining grounded in human judgment, alignment, and leadership.*

Let's talk about the elephant in every strategy room right now: AI.

It's everywhere. It's powerful. And it's moving fast.

So let's get one thing straight up front. AI is neither your enemy (at least right now!) nor your strategy.

It's a tool. A brilliant, scalable, game-changing tool.

But like any tool, its value is determined by the clarity, intention, and skill of the person using it—and the inputs you give it.

And that is why this chapter exists.

Because if you're reading this book, if you're exploring the ***InnoMagination*** framework—you're already thinking deeper. You're looking beyond shortcuts. You're trying to build something that lasts.

AI doesn't eliminate the need for strategy. It multiplies your productivity and the impact of the strategy you develop.

What AI CAN do for you:

- Surface trends faster than your analyst team
- Generate content in seconds
- Simulate customer conversations, feedback, and opinions
- Scan competitors, map markets, and analyze feedback at scale

Basically, it CAN replace an analyst or a lower-level consultant at a top firm.

What it CANNOT do:

- Decide which idea is worth pursuing for you
- Build team alignment or executive buy-in
- Manage change and collaboration within and across teams
- Spot the right hidden market opportunity based on personal

strategic intuition, organizational experience, and pattern recognition

- Create YOUR strategy (AI can help you but don't outsource your thinking to it)
- Lead and inspire your teams

AI doesn't know your customers or have a relationship with them. It doesn't know your culture. And it definitely doesn't know the nuances of your constraints. The human element—the soul of your organization—cannot be replaced.

AI needs a framework and filters...plus YOU.

That's how ***InnoMagination*** helps you leverage AI to drive innovation and revenue.

Where AI Fits Inside the *InnoMagination* Framework

SEE: Use AI to clarify what's changing
AI tools can help you identify overlooked insights, analyze voice-of-the-customer data, and spot emerging trends. Use it to:

- Research the Landscape and Market
- Summarize customer feedback across platforms
- Map competitive positioning in seconds
- Explore shifting customer behavior and unmet needs

SPARK: Use AI to expand your ideation

Once you've spotted the opportunity, AI can help you brainstorm, remix, and reframe:

- Generate naming options for repackaged offerings
- Explore alternate positioning angles
- Create quick "what if" scenarios for internal pitches
- Build financial models

DO: Use AI to remove friction and accelerate execution

This is where AI can really shine, IF pointed in the right direction:

- Draft internal communications, pitch decks, or cross-functional updates
- Create first-pass messaging or landing page copy for pilots
- Simulate customer objections and refine your narrative

But Here's the Warning Label

AI makes it easy to do **more** faster.

But MORE isn't the goal. BETTER, CLEARER, and MORE ALIGNED is.

Without a clear strategy, AI just helps you move in the wrong direction, only faster.

Without ***InnoMagination***, you risk automating noise instead of unlocking potential value. It is not only possible (but extremely likely) you will end up with more questions and less clarity if you do not have a path to follow at the start.

Why You Still Need a Human

Let me be blunt. You can't completely AI your way to an effective *InnoMagined* revenue and implementation strategy. You still need a human to:

- Spot the precise high-leverage opportunities AI can't see
- Facilitate the hard cross-functional conversations AI can't have
- Build alignment AI can't manufacture
- Push past politics, fear, and inertia.

These are (as of now) AI-free zones, every one of them.

That's where a strategic human thinker comes in. It is important to use the framework to help you drive smart, fast, collaborative ***InnoMagination***, and yes, also use AI to speed things up. But ***never*** to replace what matters.

Practical Ways to Use AI in Your *InnoMagination* Journey

Here are a few basic starter prompt concepts to use with your team. (They require feeding your AI tools enough org background material first to be useful in the exercise.) You should certainly create a library of your own prompts once you develop ones that fit your organization specifically.

- "What customer problems are we already solving that could translate to new markets?"

- "Summarize the last 100 customer reviews and identify themes."
- "Generate 10 ways to reposition [Product X] for [Audience Y]."
- "What trends are emerging in [industry] that align with our existing capabilities?"
- "What objections might a B2G buyer have about this repositioned offer?"

Use AI to support your thinking, not replace it.

AI is the Tool, You are the Leader

AI isn't the enemy of ***InnoMagination***. But it's not the leader of it, either.

YOU are.

And with the right framework, the right focus, and the right support, AI can help you move faster, scale smarter, and unlock more value than ever before.

But don't mistake the tool for the work.

InnoMagination gives you the blueprint.
Your team brings the belief.
Together, you can build the future.

Reflection Prompts for Leaders

Use these prompts to turn insight into action:

- Where in our ***InnoMagination*** process could AI add clarity and accelerate insights? Where might it risk creating noise or distraction?

- Have we clearly identified the boundaries where AI enhances our strategic thinking versus where it undermines our human intuition and judgment?

- What specific tasks, currently consuming significant time or resources, could we delegate to AI, freeing our team to focus on deeper strategic work?

- How will we ensure AI-supported ideas and initiatives maintain alignment with our organizational values, culture, and strategic vision?

- How can we actively shape our teams' mindsets so they see AI as a collaborative accelerator rather than a replacement or threat?

Fifteen

Igniting Growth: Your Call to Action

"The way to get started is to quit talking and begin doing."

— Walt Disney

Chapter Objective: *Inspire decisive action by reinforcing* ***InnoMagination™*** *as a practical, repeatable system for growth, urging leaders to move from insight to implementation with urgency, clarity, and confidence using the SEE. SPARK. DO. framework.*

THIS is YOUR Spark. Now go build the fire.

You made it. You've just completed ***InnoMaginate!: Turn Yesterday's Products into Tomorrow's Revenue,*** and I want you to pause. Not to wrap things up, but to mark the beginning of what comes next.

This isn't just a book. It is a shift in perspective. A call to ***InnoMaginate*** what's already yours, and to do it in a way that's fast, focused, and aligned with your business.

It's time to move from concept to clarity. From hesitation to action.

InnoMagination doesn't come from ***having more***. It comes from ***Seeing more*** clearly, ***Sparking more*** confidently, and ***Doing more*** intentionally.

Let's Bring It Back Full Circle: See. Spark. Do.

SEE.

You've learned how to look differently at what already exists—your products, your people, your positioning. You now know how to identify untapped value hiding in plain sight. You see decline not as a signal to retreat, but as a prompt to renew.

SPARK.

You've reconnected to purpose. You've sparked insight, alignment, and belief, inside yourself and inside your teams. You've lit a match under the myths and inertia that kept you stuck and replaced them with strategies that move you forward.

DO.

Now, it's time to act. Not perfectly. Not all at once. Just deliberately.

One product. One team. One experiment. One bold step at a time.

What You Now Know

- Decline is not inevitable. Renewal is a choice. A discipline. A strategy.
- ***Legacy Lock*** is real but not permanent. You can shift the system. You now have a blueprint.

- Your competitors won't wait. Your customers are evolving. And your relevance is earned in each decision you make from here.
- ***InnoMagination*** is your engine for renewal. It doesn't require disruption; it requires intention.
- ***InnoMagination*** is not a department. It's a discipline. It's not a side project, it is strategy.

And the best part?

You don't need to start from scratch. Everything you need is already within reach.

Your Next Moves

Start small. Start smart. Move. NOW.

- Follow the process:
    - Reconnect with your *Core Essence,* your latent assets, and your IDENTITY
    - Research the LANDSCAPE and gather data
    - Identify unmet needs in the MARKETPLACE
    - Strategically evaluate opportunities for PURSUIT
    - Create an aligned OFFERING and business case with a GTM plan

- Empower your teams, launch, measure progress, iterate as you go, and scale

InnoMagination is not an abstract ambition. It's a series of practical, powerful steps you now know how to take.

Let This Be Your New Operating Rhythm
See. Spark. Do. isn't a one-time mantra. It's a method.

It's how you create clarity, build belief, and take action, over and over again.

Let it guide how you lead, how you innovate, and how you grow.

Today is that day.
Choose to take the lead in strategy.
Choose to step into the possibilities of what Marketing **COULD** be and do.
Choose to insert yourself at the front of the line and take your seat at the table.

That's what real renewal requires today:

1. The courage to see what others miss.

2. The creativity to spark new value from what's already there.

3. The urgency to do what needs to be done, before someone else does it first.

So...what's stopping you?

We've dismantled the myths around innovation.

You've got the mindset, the method, and the map.

Now it's time to move.

Be bold. Be clear. Be in motion.

InnoMaginate!

Wishing you every success,
Traci

FUTURE YOU IS WATCHING...

Imagine it's six months from now.

You've finished this book. You had the spark. You saw the possibilities.

But you didn't act.

Now imagine your competitor did.

They repackaged. Repositioned. Captured the very market need you identified—but didn't move on.

That could have been you.

Don't let this be another missed moment.

Start today—while the insight is fresh, the opportunity is clear, and the momentum is yours for the taking.

In Case You Missed It...

SEE WHAT IT IS REALLY COSTING YOU TO WAIT

Scan the QR code to access the ***InnoMagination*** Cost of Inaction Estimator

Instantly calculate:

- Missed revenue
- Hidden support costs
- Churn and internal drag
- Your path to ROI with the under-leveraged assets already in your business

Don't guess. *Quantify* it.

claroti.com/cost-of-inaction

Sixteen

From Framework to Category

"A well-formed market category surrounds a need/problem and defines it with remarkable (and comforting) lucidity. That clarity inherently drives demand. When something or someone defines our problem better than we have seen it defined before, or uncovers an existing problem that we never fully saw or understood, our natural inclination is to want to solve that problem - and our assumption is that the one who best defined the problem must hold the best solution. That assumption is an incredibly powerful market force."

—John Farkas, Golden Spiral

Reimagining Not Just Products, But Position

Let me leave you with one final idea, one that's been present throughout this book, even if I didn't say it outright:

InnoMagination isn't just a process. It's a category-changer.

- When you reframe how innovation happens...
- When you redefine the role of Marketing as a proactive driver of growth...

- When you teach leaders to unlock value from what they already have instead of chasing something new...

You're not just solving a problem.
You're giving it a name.
You're creating a movement.
You're building a new mental shelf in the minds of your customers.
That's what category creators do.

What Category Creation Really Means

Category creation isn't about inventing something flashy.

It's about naming a new lens through which people see their existing challenges and then leading them through it with clarity and conviction.

The process:

- You identify a problem people feel but haven't yet defined
- You give it language
- You offer a structured way forward
- And you position yourself, not just as a solution, but as the authority in this new space

That's exactly what ***InnoMagination*** does.

Why This Matters Now

AI, economic and policy shifts, and general world chaos are creating constant noise and everyone is desperate for clarity.

No one really needs more content or another playbook. We're all overloaded with information as it is.

But we ALL need a new way of thinking. One that gives us permission to stop chasing shiny objects and start unlocking what's right in front of us.

When you apply ***InnoMagination***, you're not just launching new **value**.

- You're re-positioning your company.
- You're creating competitive separation.
- You're giving your market a new story to believe in.

That's the essence of category leadership.

What's Next for You as a Leader

Now that you've explored the framework, ask yourself:

- What if your business isn't just stuck on innovation? What if it's stuck on positioning?
- What if the reason your products feel tired isn't because they are, but because the category they live in is saturated or outdated?
- What would it look like to create a new space for your solution to live and lead?

Whether you're in B2C, B2B, B2G, or even DTC, the same truth applies:

> ***If you don't define the category, someone else will. And odds are, they won't tell the story in a way that serves your strengths.***

Last Thoughts: *InnoMaginate* Your New Category

I created ***InnoMagination*** to spark practical innovation.

But as I've watched leaders apply it, I've realized:

- It doesn't just reimagine products.
- It repositions companies.
- It reshapes industries.
- It redefines relevance.

You're not here to compete.
You're here to create.
So go out and ***InnoMaginate.***

Not just your offerings.

Your entire category.

Acknowledgements

First things first. Thanks to my Creator who makes all things possible.

Thank you to my husband, Mark, and to all my children (Tyler & Shannon, Raquel, Trevor & Adriana, Alanna, and Dani & Noah, and my 'adopted' one, Katie Junge) for encouraging and inspiring me to do this and to not 'die with my song still in me'.

Thank you immensely to the Claroti team who has had faith in this concept from the beginning. To Carley Trotman for generously sharing her expertise to polish the change management model for ***InnoMaginate!***; to Adriana Beltran for her support in all the details required to take this book to market; to John Jeremiah for his messaging strategy support and his long-standing faith in me; to Justin Colley for 'the hard conversations' and feedback; to Randy Billingsley for his early belief in Claroti; to Lana Bian for early reading and publicity support; and to Mark Robinson who lives and breathes this daily with me.

Huge gratitude to Beth Ladd who has been the sounding board for this book for years and who served as an editor in multiple ways, always providing incredible insights into how best to approach the casting of this vision. Thank you to Sharon Payne Young for her early belief in Claroti and for her keen insight that saved my life so many years ago.

I'm also deeply grateful to the other early readers and beloved supporters, including Amy & Marc Kriz, Nushi & Mario Carrera, Nicole Antar, Jeff & Mary Schaeffer, Dr. Tamara Baker, Dr. Charles Corprew, Robin Claterbaugh, and Dayna Jackson.

I cannot seem to find the right words to express my gratitude to my personal development coach, the priceless Viviana Torralba, for pushing me when I didn't think I could continue, and also bringing the focus to this whole project while keeping me grounded and moving forward. You'll just have to feel me sending heartwaves to you long distance!

To my mentors Claude Mitchell, who gave me the motivation and the wings to be able to ***InnoMaginate*** the first time and the freedom and the space to explore the unknown; Martha Lloyd, who unfailingly tells it to me straight but with grace, wisdom, and clarity; and Sid Sijbrandij for his advice and guidance on category creation. Thank you all. You've had more lasting impact than you can possibly imagine.

Special thanks to Denis Condon who saw potential in me that I hadn't yet recognized and who launched my career by inspiring me to bet on myself.

To my former leaders who have helped raise me up and imparted priceless wisdom, strength and inspiration: Julie Sweet, Ron Ash, Janine Cornecelli, Elaine Turville, Marty Rodgers, Karl Dedolph IV, Kate Abrey, Chris Zinner, Jake Brody, Ashish Kuthiala, Mark Rogge, Todd Barr, Stella Treas, Penny Mitchell, John Zavitsanos, Dave Garvis, Howard Woolley, Mike Maiorana, and John Peeler.

And to Mildred Winfrey, Karen & Rachel, Stacie DeGoldsby, the Honorable Vivian Henderson, Bradley Heard, Esq., Brydai Sumpter, Sharon & Steve Gammill-Kelley, and Kiris & Gary Powell, who lovingly think that I can do anything. Your amazing belief in me is both humbling and inspiring. Thank you!

There have been so many people who have contributed to this work and my life in countless other ways and I thank you all from the bottom of my heart. Please forgive me if I failed to mention you by name...I'll catch you on the next version.

InnoMagination™ Glossary of Terms

Agile Methodology: An iterative, flexible approach to innovation or product development that emphasizes collaboration, speed, continuous improvement, and customer feedback.

Brand Equity: The value of a brand in the marketplace, based on consumer perception, recognition, and trust.

CAC (Customer Acquisition Cost): The total cost of acquiring a new customer, including marketing, sales, and onboarding expenses.

Change Management: A structured approach to transitioning individuals, teams, and organizations to a desired future state, especially during innovation or transformation efforts.

Change Readiness Assessment: A tool to evaluate how prepared individuals or teams are to engage with and sustain change initiatives.

Collaboration Check: A structured check-in at key phases of the **InnoMagination™** process to align stakeholders, confirm progress, and ensure cross-functional clarity.

Core Essence*:** The strategic DNA of an organization, defined by its mission, values, brand promise, personality, and market perception—used to anchor ***InnoMagination decisions.

CSAT (Customer Satisfaction Score): A metric that measures how satisfied customers are with a product or service, often used to track customer experience performance.

Cross-Functional Pod: A small, agile team composed of individuals from multiple departments working together toward a shared ***InnoMagination*** goal.

CXO: A general term for C-level executives (e.g., CEO, CMO, CGO, CRO, CIO, CTO, CPO, CSO, COO, CFO, etc.) responsible for enterprise-level leadership and strategy.

Digital Transformation: The integration of digital technologies into all areas of a business, fundamentally changing how it operates and delivers value to customers.

DO. (from SEE. SPARK. DO.): The final phase in the **InnoMagination™** rhythm—focused on execution, action, and measurable results based on strategy and insight.

DRASCI Matrix: A tool used to define roles and responsibilities across ***InnoMagination*** initiatives: Driver, Responsible, Accountable, Support, Consulted, Informed.

Ecosystem Interdependencies: The broader network of platforms, partners, systems, and processes that are impacted by or contribute to a product or service offering.

Feature Creep: The excessive addition of features to a product that increases complexity without adding real value.

GTM (Go-To-Market) Strategy: A cross-functional plan for how an offering will be positioned, launched, sold, and supported in the market.

Innovation-as-a-Discipline: The mindset that ***InnoMagination*** is not a one-time event or department—it's a repeatable, measurable, strategic process embedded in business operations.

***InnoMagination* Culture:** An environment that fosters curiosity, risk-taking, collaboration, and continuous improvement across all levels of the organization.

Innovation Ecosystem: The interconnected network of tools, platforms, people, and processes that support innovation within an organization.

Innovation Inertia: The internal resistance to change caused by outdated systems, fear, or cultural norms that favor the status quo.

Innovation Theater: Surface-level innovation activities (like adding features or launching hackathons that do no result in a launched product) that give the appearance of progress without real impact.

InnoMagination *TM*: A framework that guides organizations to unlock growth by reimagining and repositioning existing products, assets, and capabilities.

InnoMagination Asset Category Matrix: A tool used to evaluate and categorize ***InnoMagination*** opportunities based on their alignment with *Core Essence* and potential market impact.

InnoMagined Asset / Rediscovered Asset: An existing product, service, or capability reimagined to deliver new value in a different market or context.

InnoMagination Coach or Consultant: A trained expert who facilitates the implementation of the ***InnoMagination™*** framework within an organization.

Innovation Lab: A separate team within an organization tasked with exploring breakthrough ideas outside the constraints of daily operations.

Iterate (from Measure & Iterate Loop): The process of refining a product or idea based on customer feedback and performance data after launch.

Latent / Dormant Asset: An under-leveraged, under-monetized existing product, service, or capability within an organization.

Legacy Lock Contradiction: The tension that arises when organizations seek innovation but maintain systems and structures that prevent change.

Market Gap: An underserved or unaddressed area of customer need that presents an opportunity for growth or differentiation.

Marketing Powered Innovation (MPI): The approach to innovation using the ***InnoMagination*** framework where Marketing leads by using deep customer insight, market intelligence, and storytelling to uncover and activate growth opportunities.

Measure & Iterate Loop: A continuous cycle of launching, measuring, learning, and refining a product or initiative to improve results and relevance.

MVP (Minimum Viable Product): The simplest version of a product that can be released to test assumptions, gather feedback, and validate demand.

NPS (Net Promoter Score): A metric that measures customer loyalty and likelihood to recommend a product or service to others.

OKRs (Objectives and Key Results): A goal-setting methodology used to align teams around measurable outcomes and strategic priorities.

Opportunity Assessment Wheel: A scoring tool used within the **InnoMagination™** framework to evaluate opportunities across six key dimensions: ROI, market fit, risk, alignment, speed-to-market, and change readiness.

Organizational Inertia Audit: A diagnostic tool used to identify cultural, structural, or leadership barriers that may be slowing ***InnoMagination*** momentum.

Pilot Launch: A limited, controlled release of a product or service to test effectiveness and gather insights before a full-scale launch.

PMO (Project Management Office): A centralized team that oversees project execution, timelines, and resource allocation across the enterprise.

Product-Market Fit: The degree to which a product satisfies a real market need, often used as a threshold for scaling.

Recombinant Innovation: The creation of new value by combining existing assets, ideas, or capabilities in original ways; the foundation of the ***InnoMagination****™* concept.

RevOps (Revenue Operations): A strategic function that aligns Sales, Marketing, and Customer Success operations to drive predictable revenue growth.

ROMI (Return on Marketing Investment): A measure of the revenue generated from marketing activities relative to the cost of those activities.

SEE. (from SEE. SPARK. DO.): The first key in the ***InnoMagination™*** **process**—focused on recognizing hidden value, market shifts, and opportunity in existing assets.

SEE. SPARK. DO. The core rhythm of the ***InnoMagination™*** framework: SEE opportunities, SPARK belief and clarity, DO the work that drives results.

Siloed Teams / Silos: Departments or groups that operate independently from one another, often leading to inefficiency, misalignment, or duplicated efforts.

Skunkworks: An unofficial or autonomous group within a company that works on advanced or unconventional projects.

SPARK (from SEE. SPARK. DO.): The second key in the ***InnoMagination™*** **process**—focused on igniting belief, insight, and collaborative momentum.

Stakeholder Map: A tool that identifies and categorizes stakeholders by their level of influence and impact to tailor engagement and communication strategies accordingly.

Strategic Alignment Checklist: A tool used to ensure that

InnoMagination initiatives align with the organization's core values, mission, brand, and priorities.

Strategic Wedge: A focused, manageable starting point (team, product, or segment) used to pilot and prove new ***InnoMagination*** strategies before scaling.

TAM (Total Addressable Market): The total market demand available for a product or service, used as one measure of potential opportunity size.

Test & Refine: A rapid feedback process used to test prototypes or early versions of an offering, then refine based on input and learning.

Value Proposition: A clear statement of the benefit a product or service delivers to a specific customer segment, and why it's better than alternatives.

Vanity Metrics: Surface-level metrics that may look impressive (e.g., pageviews, likes, followers) but don't meaningfully reflect business impact or strategic success.

White Space: An unexplored or underserved market segment where unmet needs exist—often the source of high-growth opportunities.

Bibliography

[1] Sims, Peter. Little Bets: How Breakthrough Ideas Emerge from Small Discoveries. Simon & Schuster, 2013.

[2] Anthony, Scott D. "How to Bring an Entrepreneurial Mindset to Your Organization." Harvard Business Review, 23 May 2017, https://hbr.org/2017/05/how-to-bring-an-entrepreneurial-mindset-to-your-organization.

[3] Accenture. "Pulse of Change: 2024 Index." Jan. 2024, www.accenture.com/content/dam/accenture/final/accenture-com/document-2/Accenture-Pulse-of-Change-2024-Index-Executive-Summary.pdf.

[4] Vistage Worldwide, Inc. "CEO Confidence Index Report Q2 2024: Focus on Artificial Intelligence." July 2024, www.vistage.com/research-center/business-financials/economic-trends/20240716-ceo- confidence-dips-q2-vistage-ceo-index/.

[5] PwC. "PwC's 27th Annual Global CEO Survey: Thriving in an Age of Continuous Reinvention." Jan. 2024, www.pwc.com/gx/en/ceo-survey/2024/download/27th-ceo-survey.pdf.

[6] Adobe Systems Incorporated. "Adobe Reports Record Quarterly and Annual Revenue." 13 Dec. 2012, www.adobe.com/content/dam/cc/en/investor-relations/pdfs/Q412Earnings.pdf.

[7] Adobe Inc. "Adobe Reports Record Q4 and Fiscal 2020 Revenue." 10 Dec. 2020, www.adobe.com/cc-shared/assets/investor-relations/pdfs/a7b36fmf92v6f.pdf.

[8] Deloitte. "The Multiple Roles of the 21st-Century Chief Marketing Officer." Deloitte US, 2025, https://www2.deloitte.com/us/en/pages/chief-marketing-officer/articles/roles-of-the-cmo.htm.

[9] "The Top Priorities And Challenges Of CMOs In 2024: Report." *The CMO*, 28 May 2024, thecmo.com/career/priorities-of-cmos-2024/.

[10] "5 Biggest Challenges for CMOs in 2024 [With Proof]." CodeSM Marketing, codesm.marketing/blog/biggest-challenges-cmos-2024/.

[11] "Economic Optimism Doubles, yet Almost Half of CEOs Do Not Believe Their Businesses Will Be Viable in a Decade as Tech and Climate Pressures Accelerate: PwC Global CEO Survey." PwC, 15 Jan. 2024, www.pwc.com/gx/en/news-room/press-releases/2024/economic-optimism-doubles-yet-almost-half-of-ceos-do-not-believe-their-businesses-will-be-viable-in-a-decade.html.

[12] Tiwari, Namita. "The Top Five Challenges For CMOs." Forbes, 26 July 2024, www.forbes.com/councils/forbescommunicationscouncil/2024/07/26/t

he-top-five-challenges-for-cmos/.

[13] Spencer Stuart. "CMO Tenure Study 2025: The Evolution of Marketing Leadership." Spencer Stuart, Mar. 2025, www.spencerstuart.com/research-and-insight/cmo-tenure-study-2025-the-evolution-of- marketing-leadership.

[14] Gartner, Inc. "Gartner Survey Reveals Only 45% of CMOs Surpass Senior Executive Expectations Despite Achieving Objectives." Gartner Newsroom, 25 Feb. 2025, www.gartner.com/en/newsroom/press-releases/ 2025-02-24-gartner-survey-reveals-only-45-percent-of-cmos-surpass-senior-executive-expectations-despite-achieving-objectives.

[15] Silva, Bernardo, and Michael Hunter. "Driving Growth Through Accountability - The Role Of The Chief Growth Officer." Mondaq, 9 Mar. 2023, www.mondaq.com/unitedstates/shareholders/1291486/driving-growth-through-accountability-the-role-of-the-chief-growth-officer.

[16] Seuss, Dr. Oh, the Places You'll Go!. Random House, 1990.

[17] Rayl, Ali. "Becoming Slack: The Story of a Son of a Glitch." SitePoint, 4 Feb. 2016, www.sitepoint.com/slack-story-son-glitch/.

[18] "Corning's Journey From Cookware To Gorilla Glass." NPR, 14 Mar. 2011, www.npr.org/2011/03/14/134240989/cornings-journey-from-cookware-to-gorilla-glass.

[19] "Big Blue's Big Bet: How IBM Transformed Itself for the Age of AI and Cloud." CFI.co, 22 Apr. 2025,

www.cfi.co/northamerica/2025/04/big-blues-big-bet-how-ibm-transformed-itself-for- the-age-of-ai-and-cloud/.

[20] "Who We Are: American Express History, Values, & Vision." American Express, www.americanexpress.com/en-us/company/who-we-are/.

[21] Taylor, Kate. "How Chipotle Became One Of America's Most Successful Brands." Forbes, 29 Mar. 2021, www.forbes.com/sites/katetaylor/2021/03/29/how-chipotle-became-one-of-americas-most-successful-brands/.

[22] Weiss, Suzannah. "The Accidental Invention of Play-Doh." Smithsonian Magazine, 12 Nov. 2019, www.smithsonianmag.com/innovation/accidental-invention-play-doh-180973527/.

[23] Contrary Research. "Report: Sword Health Business Breakdown & Founding Story." Contrary Research, 7 Mar. 2025, research.contrary.com/company/sword-health.

[24] "About." Second Order Effects, 1 Oct. 2024, soeffects.com/about.

[25] "Able: Home | Building Software with World-Class Talent and AI." Able, 2024, www.able.co.

[26] Repko, Melissa. "HHGregg throws in the towel, will close all 220 stores." Retail Dive, 10 Apr. 2017, www.retaildive.com/news/hhgregg-throws-in-the-towel-will-close-all-220-stores/440108/.

[27] Repko, Melissa. "Stein Mart files for bankruptcy with plans to liquidate its stores." Retail Dive, 12 Aug. 2020,

www.retaildive.com/news/stein-mart-files-for-bankruptcy-with-plans-to-liquidate- its-stores/583376/.

[28] Hanbury, Mary. "Pier 1 Stores Closing: How the Retailer Had a Rise and Fall." Business Insider, 18 Feb. 2020, www.businessinsider.com/pier-1-stores-history-rise-and-fall-2020-1.

[29] "Thomas Cook collapse: The seven signs it will happen to your business." IMD, 24 Sept. 2019, www.imd.org/research-knowledge/digital/articles/thomas-cook-collapse-the-seven-signs-it-will-happen-to-your-business/.

[30] Sandu, Bogdan. "What Happened to Pan Am? A Tale of Its Bankruptcy." TMS Outsource, 21 Apr. 2025, tms-outsource.com/blog/posts/what-happened-to-pan-am/.

[31] Goodman, Matthew. "Gadget giant Sharper Image files for bankruptcy." CNN Money, 20 Feb. 2008, money.cnn.com/2008/02/20/smbusiness/sharper_image_bankruptcy.fs b/.

[32] Repko, Melissa. "Gymboree files bankruptcy for 2nd time in 2 years." Retail Dive, 17 Jan. 2019, www.retaildive.com/news/gymboree-files-bankruptcy-for-2nd-time-in-2-years/546295/.

[33] "The Downfall of Sears: A Failure to Embrace Digital Transformation." Cleo, www.cleo.com/blog/downfall-of-sears.

[34] "Compaq." Britannica Money, 29 Apr. 2025, www.britannica.com/money/Compaq.

[35] "Why did Yahoo Fail? The Rise and Fall of a Dot-Com Tech Giant." EM360Tech, 17 Feb. 2025, www.em360tech.com/tech-articles/why-did-yahoo-fail-rise-and-fall-dot-com-tech-giant.

[36] "RadioShack: Failure to Innovate in a Digital World." Reidel Law Firm, 10 July 2023, reidellawfirm.com/radioshack-failure-to-innovate-in-a-digital-world/.

[37] "The Fall of BlackBerry: How Ignoring Innovation Led to Decline." Time for Designs, 10 Oct. 2023, www.timefordesigns.com/blog/2023/10/10/the-fall-of-blackberry-how-ignoring-innovation-led-to-decline/.

[38] Sandu, Bogdan. "A Retailer Out of Game: What Happened to Sports Authority?" TMS Outsource, 21 Apr. 2025, tms-outsource.com/blog/posts/what-happened-to-sports-authority/.

[39] "Bios - Recombinant Innovation." Recombinant Innovation, 1 Apr. 2017, http://rinucleus.com/bios/

[40] Drucker, Peter F. "The Discipline of Innovation." Harvard Business Review, vol. 63, no. 3, May–June 1985, pp. 67–72.

[41] Christensen, Clayton M. The Innovator's Dilemma: When New Technologies Cause Great Firms to Fail. Harvard Business School Press, 1997.

[42] Day, George S. Market Driven Strategy: Processes for Creating Value. Free Press, 1990.

[43] Weiss, Suzannah. "How the Reese's Peanut Butter Cup Became

America's Favorite Candy." Smithsonian Magazine, 27 Oct. 2021, www.smithsonianmag.com/innovation/how-the-reeses-peanut-butter-cup- became-americas-favorite-candy-180978896/.

[44] "Rollaboard: A Brief History of Rolling Luggage." Travelpro, www.travelpro.com/blogs/the-travelpro-blog/the-history-of-rolling-luggage.

[45] "Experience-led Growth: A New Way to Create Value." McKinsey & Company, 23 Mar. 2023, www.mckinsey.com/capabilities/growth-marketing-and-sales/our-insights/experience-led-growth-a-new-way-to-create-value.

[46] Gasparro, Annie. "How Nerds Gummy Clusters Became America's Top Halloween Candy." The Wall Street Journal, 30 Oct. 2023, www.wsj.com/business/media/nerds-gummy-clusters-candy-halloween-35ae2e2a.

[47] Sean. "What Baking Soda Was Originally Used For – Product Positioning." NxtStep, 10 Dec. 2019, nxtstep.io/blog/baking-soda-product-positioning/.

[48] Denning, Steve. "How Amazon Became One of America's Most Beloved Brands." Harvard Business Review, 28 Sept. 2018, hbr.org/2018/09/how-amazon-became-one-of-americas-most-beloved-brands.

[49] "LEGO Takes Customers' Innovations Further." MIT Sloan Management Review, 12 Sept. 2023, sloanreview.mit.edu/article/lego-takes-customers-innovations-further/.

[50] "About Us." Zappos.com, www.zappos.com/c/about.

[51] "Netflix Content Recommendation System – Product Analytics Case Study." HelloPM, 16 July 2024, hellopm.co/netflix-content-recommendation-system-product-analytics-case-study/.

[52] Singi, Angad. "How Apple Keeps Its Customers Satisfied Always?" Marketer.club, 9 Jan. 2025, www.marketer.club/p/how-apple-keeps-its-customers-satisfied-always.

[53] "Galaxy S9 Developers Share 9 Key Focuses That Shaped the Device's Design." Samsung Newsroom, 24 Apr. 2018, news.samsung.com/global/galaxy-s9-developers-share-9-key-focuses-that-shaped-the- devices-design.

[54] "BlackBerry's Decline: A Case Study in the Smartphone Market's Rapid Evolution." Cognitive Market Research, 21 Mar. 2025, www.cognitivemarketresearch.com/blog/blackberry-s-decline-a-case-study-in-the-smartphone-market-s-rapid-evolution.

[55] "Spanx Information." RocketReach, 2025, rocketreach.co/spanx-profile_b5c7bf59f42e0d4a.

[56] Vajre, Sangram, and Bryan Brown. MOVE: The 4-Question Go-to-Market Framework. Lioncrest Publishing, 2021.

[57] "Using All the Features: Beating the 80/20 Rule with Customer Training." Litmos Blog, 26 Feb. 2025, www.litmos.com/blog/articles/using-all-the-features-beating-the-80-20-rule-with-customer-training.

AFTERWORD

Examples of *InnoMagination* 'in the Wild'

There are so many case studies about organizations that have used *InnoMaginative* thinking to transform, I couldn't include them all. However, I still want to share some additional inspiration, so please enjoy the following stories that I have previously posted on LinkedIn in my *"Textbook Tuesdays"* series.

I hope they help you SEE what is possible for your organization, to SPARK fresh ideas so that you are inspired to DO what it takes to drive the revenue you need.

Apple iPhone

Everyone thinks Apple is THE innovation company because they INVENTED the future. That's not really what happened.

Apple became the most valuable company on earth because they repeatedly REIMAGINED what they already owned.

They didn't invent new every time. They leveraged what they had and made it better.

For some strange reason, most companies believe innovation only counts if it's brand new.

When growth slows, they immediately start building new products or developing new capabilities. It can take years, cost millions, and come with zero guarantees.

Apple proved the opposite.

- iPod → built from acquired SoundJam software (peaked at 50% of Apple's revenue)
- iTunes → evolved from music manager to content ecosystem
- iPhone → iPod Touch + phone capability (now generates $209B+ annually)

Result: Each generation built on the last

The iPod taught them hardware and user experience.

iTunes taught them ecosystem lock-in. (!!!)

The iPod Touch became the iPhone prototype.

By 2007, Apple had already spent years perfecting the components. They just combined them differently.

The innovation wasn't the invention. It was SEEING how existing assets could become something bigger.

You're sitting on technology, relationships, data, and capabilities that could be repositioned or recombined. But because it's not "new," it doesn't feel like innovation.

But think about this:

- What did you build in the past that could be the foundation for today?
- What acquisition could be integrated into your core offering?
- What capability are you dismissing as "old" that just needs a little reimagining?

If Apple can turn a music player into a $209B annual revenue stream by building on what they already owned, what could you do with your portfolio?

YouTube®

In 2006, YouTube was hemorrhaging money, drowning in copyright lawsuits, and had zero monetization strategy. Most companies looked at it and saw a liability. A video platform burning cash with no clear path to profitability.

Google saw it differently. YouTube wasn't broken. It was just missing the right capabilities.

YouTube had massive traffic and cultural relevance. Google had the ad technology, the infrastructure to handle the scale, and the expertise to solve copyright chaos. Neither company could have built what the other had—but together, they became unstoppable.

- Money-losing platform → $29B+ annual revenue
- Copyright lawsuits → Content ID system (industry standard)
- Standalone site → integrated with Google's ad network and cloud infrastructure

Google paid $1.65B in 2006. By 2023, YouTube generated over $29 billion in annual revenue. That's a 1,757% ROI...and that's just advertising, not counting Premium, TV, or Music subscriptions.

YouTube didn't get "fixed." It got MATCHED with the right strengths.

Sometimes, you acquire assets that underperform, and everyone assumes the asset is the problem. But often, the acquisition isn't broken. It's just not matched with the capabilities you already own...

You have the sales channel. Or the customer base. Or the technology infrastructure. Or the domain expertise. The answer is already in your portfolio. You just haven't connected the dots yet.

What have you acquired that's underperforming? What strengths do you already have that could transform it?

Sometimes you don't need to fix the asset. You just need to find a partner.

The Cabo San Lucas Fire Station

While walking down a street in Cabo San Lucas, Mexico, my husband and I passed a fire station. What I saw next stopped me in my tracks.

Signs requesting donations? Sure, I expected that.

But next to the station was an entire storefront selling Cabo Fire Department T-shirts, hats, and water bottles. Full-on branded merchandise! At a fire station?!?

I was so impressed, I turned around and went back to take a photo.

Here's the context: The Cabo Fire Department is a volunteer organization founded in 1982 by one person with buckets, radios, and an old vehicle. Since government funding doesn't cover their needs, they've always relied on donations.

But at some point, someone asked: "What do we already have that people would pay for?"

They looked at their assets:

- A recognizable brand (firefighters are universally respected)
- A tourist destination location (because people want Cabo-branded souvenirs)
- High foot traffic (tourists walking past constantly)
- Equipment people find interesting (fire trucks)
- Expertise companies need (safety training, inspections)

Would this work in Toledo, Ohio or Salina, Kansas? Maybe not the T-shirts. But the principle still applies. They matched WHAT THEY HAD to what their market actually WANTED.

Then they built multiple revenue streams:

- Merchandise stores at the station and mall locations
- Cold water sales at the marina ($1/bottle on cruise ship days)
- "BomberTour" (converted a 1966 fire truck into a tour bus)
- Safety training and inspections for local businesses
- Water delivery using existing trucks

They didn't wait for a grant and they didn't build new capabilities. They looked at what they already owned and asked, "How else could this create value?"

If a volunteer fire department in Mexico can turn their trucks into a tour business and their brand into a merchandise line, what could your organization do (even if it is a non-profit)?

You already have assets people would pay for. You just haven't thought of them that way yet.

The Cabo Fire Department figured it out with buckets and an old truck. What's stopping you?

Marvel + Disney

In 2009, Marvel was a struggling comic book publisher. They had iconic characters but a broken business model. Print publishing was dying and they'd already sold off film rights to their best characters just to survive (Spider-Man to Sony, X-Men to Fox).

Most people saw a dying medium with its best assets already gone.

Instead, Bob Iger envisioned a cinematic universe that hadn't been built...YET.

Characters that could anchor films, theme parks, streaming platforms, and merchandise empires.

He saw:

- Struggling publisher → $30B+ box office franchise
- Fragmented licensing → integrated cinematic universe
- Print assets → Disney+ anchor content

Disney paid $4B in 2009. Since then, Marvel has generated $30B+ at the box office alone—a 750% ROI—not counting merchandise, streaming, or theme parks.

The characters didn't change. Disney just saw what Marvel COULDN'T see in themselves.

So many companies are sitting on acquisitions they don't know how to activate, or dismissing their own capabilities because they're too close to see the value.

Sometimes you need an outsider to say, "Hellloooo...do you realize what you ACTUALLY have here??"

What did you acquire that's sitting dormant?

What capability are you running that another vertical is desperate for?

Sometimes the acquirer sees value you can't.

And sometimes YOU could be the acquirer seeing what everyone else is missing. What embedded upside is waiting for you to unlock it?

Amazon → AWS

I once sold sodas in the middle of I-95. (True story.) It accidentally taught me everything about Amazon's $90B secret.

Many years ago, I was on my way to my ex's family reunion—a whole caravan of cars packed with food and ice-cold drinks headed toward Philadelphia on the 4th of July.

It was blazing hot, the kids were getting cranky, and then a serious accident shut everything down. Complete standstill. Hours of nothing moving.

At some point it became clear we weren't going to get there until late afternoon (if we were lucky), which meant we'd have way more food and drinks than we'd ever need by the time we arrived.

I looked around at a highway full of hot, stranded strangers and had an idea. I grabbed some of the kids' drawing paper, made a few signs, recruited the rest of the family, and started walking up and down the parking lot that I-95 had become, selling ice-cold drinks to anyone who'd have them.

We sold out. Completely unplanned. We made zero new investment, just matched our excess capacity to the unmet need that was sitting right in front of us.

What's this got to do with Amazon?

They did the same thing—just with 'slightly' higher stakes.

In the early 2000s, Amazon built a massive internal server infrastructure to run their e-commerce business. Smart people noticed that a lot of that capacity sat idle during off-peak periods. Most companies treat that as a cost of doing business...you build for peak demand and accept the waste. But someone at Amazon asked a different question: what if we sold it?

- Excess infrastructure → commercial product
- Idle capacity → pay-as-you-go cloud services for startups and enterprises
- Internal cost center → $90B+ annual revenue (now the most profitable division in the company)
- AWS wasn't invented from scratch. The bones were already there. They just reimagined how to use the extra capacity THEY ALREADY HAD.

What internal tool, capability, or infrastructure are you treating as overhead that another company would actually pay for? Do you have under-monetized assets you could leverage?

You've already built it. You're already running it. The market may be right outside your window, hot and waiting, and all you need is a sign.

Iceland's Blue Lagoon

Sometimes your biggest growth opportunity is literally waste.

On a recent stopover in Iceland with a visit to the Blue Lagoon (which I highly recommend, by the way), I learned this fascinating story...

In 1976, geothermal seawater from Iceland's Svartsengi power plant pooled in a lava field. They were stuck with industrial runoff nobody wanted.

Today, that water powers a skincare business growing at 130%, sold at Neiman Marcus worldwide. National Geographic calls it one of '25 Wonders of the World'.

What changed? Nothing about the water. EVERYTHING about how they saw it.

Locals bathed in it for years, noticing skin improvements, especially for psoriasis. Scientists discovered exceptionally high silica, minerals, and unique microalgae with bioactive properties.

In 1992, a physician founded Blue Lagoon Ltd. He medically validated that it worked for psoriasis treatments. By 1995, they launched skincare products as a clinical extension (not tourist souvenirs).

They eventually secured two exclusive patents and packaged three product lines for different audiences, all from the very same asset.

The brilliant part? Over 1 million annual visitors experience the brand in person, then buy it when they get home. The destination IS the demand engine. (You really should see their marketing.)

RESULT: 100% year-to-date growth across channels.

This is asset activation, matching existing capabilities to unmet needs. No new builds.

Most tech companies do the opposite. When they hit growth plateaus, they think, "Build something new." (Which generally means: 18-24 months, $2M+ investment, and massive risk.)

Meanwhile, they're sitting on dormant acquisitions, underleveraged products, and capabilities their sales teams don't sell.

The question isn't "What should we invent?" It's "What do we ALREADY own that we're not seeing?"

Blue Lagoon reimagined their industrial waste as a wonder of the world.

What are you dismissing as a byproduct that could be your next revenue stream?

Monaco

I've identified over $1B in hidden revenue opportunities in my career. This 'Monaco Playbook' is the strategy I use most.

Most people don't know this story. Which is a problem, because it's the exact blueprint B2B tech companies need right now.

1950s: Monaco was broke. The casino was losing money. Tourism was declining. No resources to "innovate."

Most consultants would say: "Build new industries. Diversify. Modernize."

But Monaco had ZERO capital to build new.

So Prince Rainier III looked at the assets they ALREADY owned:

- A struggling casino
- A tiny piece of Mediterranean coastline
- A tax structure nobody cared about
- A faded Monte Carlo brand

But then...He didn't invent something new. He reimagined.

- CASINO: Repositioned from middle-class gambling → ultra-luxury destination for the global elite

- COASTLINE: Reclaimed land from the sea, turning constraint (0.78 sq. mi) into advantage (exclusivity = highest real estate prices on earth)

- TAX STRUCTURE: Activated as competitive edge for ultra-wealthy residents

- BRAND: Leveraged his marriage to Grace Kelly, F1 Grand Prix, yacht culture

RESULT: $7.6B GDP. Today, Monaco has the highest per capita income globally...and it was built entirely from assets they already had.

This is the same approach I used at a national wireless company. I identified Public Safety as a $1B+ untapped market by matching existing network capabilities to unmet vertical needs. No new infrastructure. Just strategic repositioning of what they already owned.

Most leaders assume "We need to build something new." They think they need new products and new capabilities.

But unfortunately, this usually means an 18-24 month timeline and a $2M+ investment.

Really, the growth they need is usually ALREADY in their portfolio:

- Products not yet positioned for adjacent markets

- Acquisition assets sitting dormant

- Capabilities their sales teams don't even sell

YOU ALREADY OWN THE ASSETS.

You just can't see the 'Monaco story' in YOUR business--YET. That's where external perspective changes everything.

Want to read more case studies of *InnoMagination* in the wild? Follow me on LinkedIn to read "Textbook Tuesdays" every week: https://www.linkedin.com/in/tracirobinsonwilliams

About The Author

Traci Robinson-Williams, MBA, is a revenue growth strategist and builder of practical paths to innovation.

Over the course of her career, she's worked inside complex, leading organizations—including Verizon Wireless, GitLab, and Accenture—**where she observed a common challenge across industries: Marketing has untapped potential to drive strategic growth, but is rarely positioned to do so.** She knew there had to be a better way.

That insight led to the creation of the ***InnoMagination™*** **framework**, a repeatable, cross-functional process designed to help Marketing and Growth executives surface untapped value and activate new growth by reimagining the assets they already have in their organizations.

Traci's breakthrough came when she reframed an overlooked market opportunity, built the business case from the ground up, and led a team to build the foundation for **$1 billion in revenue from a $5 million Marketing investment**. That experience became her proofpoint…and her mission.

Today, through her company, **Claroti**, Traci helps organizations uncover hidden value, build internal alignment, and move faster on the opportunities already within reach. Her passion lies in **empowering Marketing and Growth executives** to lead innovation, not just support it.

She holds a B.S. in Business and an MBA in Global Management, with additional studies in International Marketing and Business Analytics. But what defines her most is a belief that innovation doesn't start with invention—it starts with seeing differently, asking "what if," and having the courage to lead from where you are.

Traci lives with and her husband in rural Northern Virginia and in France, whenever possible.

Ready to Turn Insights into Action?

You've read the book. You're inspired, clear, and ready to move forward.

Now, accelerate your progress with the ***InnoMagination™ Template Toolkit***, the ultimate companion to help you quickly implement what you've learned to transform your organization's middle ground (6-24 months) innovation gap.

Inside, you'll find practical, easy-to-use templates with instructions, checklists, and scripts designed specifically to:

- Quickly articulate your *Core Essence* and identify hidden assets and overlooked opportunities already within your organization
- Clearly map unmet market needs and lucrative market gaps
- Efficiently build compelling, executive-ready business cases
- Confidently position your ***InnoMagination*** initiatives for internal buy-in

No more guesswork. No more wasted time. Just clear, practical tools to rapidly turn yesterday's products into tomorrow's revenue.

Get immediate access to your ***InnoMagination™ Template Toolkit*** today:

www.claroti.com/toolkit

InnoMagination doesn't have to be complicated. But you do need the right tools.

Bring InnoMaginate! to Your Organization

Transform How Your Teams See Revenue Opportunities

InnoMaginate! equips leaders and teams with a proven framework to uncover hidden revenue inside assets they already own. Whether you're looking to spark innovation across your organization or give your team a competitive edge, this book delivers actionable insights backed by real case studies.

Bulk Orders for Teams & Organizations

Perfect for:

- Corporate and University learning & development programs
- Leadership offsites and Sales and team kickoffs
- Revenue, Marketing, and Innovation teams
- Executive book clubs

Quantity discounts available. Contact us for pricing and customization options including branded covers, team workshops, and author-signed copies.

Book Traci to Speak

Traci delivers the See. Spark. Do.™ keynote and workshops based on the InnoMaginate! methodology. Ideal for corporate events, innovation summits, revenue leadership gatherings, and strategy conferences.

Available formats:

• 45–60 minute keynote

• 30–45 minute breakout session

• Full-day workshops

Get in Touch

For bulk orders, speaking inquiries, or media requests:

traci@claroti.com

tracirobinsonwilliams.com

linkedin.com/in/tracirobinsonwilliams

www.ingramcontent.com/pod-product-compliance
Lightning Source LLC
LaVergne TN
LVHW010643110826
845149LV00014B/2939

9798999187826